Machine Learning for Data Mining

Improve your data mining capabilities with advanced predictive modeling

Jesus Salcedo

BIRMINGHAM - MUMBAI

Machine Learning for Data Mining

Commissioning Editor: Sunith Shetty
Acquisition Editor: Devika Battike
Content Development Editor: Unnati Guha
Technical Editor: Dinesh Chaudhary
Copy Editor: Safis Editing
Project Coordinator: Manthan Patel
Proofreader: Safis Editing
Indexer: Pratik Shirodkar
Graphics: Jisha Chirayil
Production Coordinator: Arvindkumar Gupta

First published: April 2019

Production reference: 1300419

Published by Packt Publishing Ltd.
Livery Place
35 Livery Street
Birmingham
B3 2PB, UK.

ISBN 978-1-83882-897-4

www.packtpub.com

Contributors

About the author

Jesus Salcedo has a PhD in psychometrics from Fordham University. He is an independent statistical consultant and has been using SPSS products for over 20 years. He is a former SPSS Curriculum Team Lead and Senior Education Specialist who has written numerous SPSS training courses and trained thousands of users.

Packt is searching for authors like you

If you're interested in becoming an author for Packt, please visit authors.packtpub.com and apply today. We have worked with thousands of developers and tech professionals, just like you, to help them share their insight with the global tech community. You can make a general application, apply for a specific hot topic that we are recruiting an author for, or submit your own idea.

`mapt.io`

Mapt is an online digital library that gives you full access to over 5,000 books and videos, as well as industry leading tools to help you plan your personal development and advance your career. For more information, please visit our website.

Why subscribe?

- Spend less time learning and more time coding with practical eBooks and Videos from over 4,000 industry professionals

- Improve your learning with Skill Plans built especially for you

- Get a free eBook or video every month

- Mapt is fully searchable

- Copy and paste, print, and bookmark content

Packt.com

Did you know that Packt offers eBook versions of every book published, with PDF and ePub files available? You can upgrade to the eBook version at `www.packt.com` and as a print book customer, you are entitled to a discount on the eBook copy. Get in touch with us at `customercare@packtpub.com` for more details.

At `www.packt.com`, you can also read a collection of free technical articles, sign up for a range of free newsletters, and receive exclusive discounts and offers on Packt books and eBooks.

Table of Contents

Preface

30% of data mining vacancies also involve machine learning. And those that do are 30% better paid than the rest. If you're involved in data mining, you need to get on top of machine learning, before it gets on top of you.

Hands-On Machine Learning for Data Mining gives you everything you need to bring the power of machine learning into your data mining work. This book will enable you to pair the best algorithms with the right tools and processes. You will see how systems can learn from data, identify patterns, and make predictions on data, all with minimal human intervention.

Who this book is for

If you are a data mining professional who wishes to get a ticket to a 30% higher salary by adding machine learning to your skill set, then this is the ideal course for you. No prior knowledge in machine learning is assumed.

What this book covers

Chapter 1, *Introducing Machine Learning Predictive Models*, introduces you to the theory behind predictive models, looking at how they work and providing an insight into types of predictive modeling, such as the neural network model, which is explained in brief in this chapter.

Chapter 2, *Getting Started with Machine Learning*, introduces you to the implementation of a neural network model, and gives an insight into the implementation of **Support Vector Machines (SVMs)** as well.

Chapter 3, *Understanding Models*, explains different types of models and the situations in which each of them should ideally be used.

Chapter 4, *Improving Individual Models*, shows you different ways in which we can improve our models. This chapter will show you four methods to improve the accuracy of your model.

Chapter 5, *Advanced Ways of Improving Models*, focuses on combining different models in different ways to get increasingly better results. In this chapter, we will see how a certain part of a dataset, which doesn't contribute much to the results of a neural network model, performs very well on the CHAID and C5.0 decision tree models. We will also see how to model the errors to prepare our models.

To get the most out of this book

- Some knowledge on what data mining is, and the basic concepts of machine learning, will act as starting points for this book.
- Familiarity with any machine learning modeler, specifically the SPSS Modeler provided by IBM, will be a plus, but isn't necessary.

Download the example code files

You can download the example code files for this book from your account at www.packt.com. If you purchased this book elsewhere, you can visit www.packt.com/support and register to have the files emailed directly to you.

You can download the code files by following these steps:

1. Log in or register at www.packt.com.
2. Select the **SUPPORT** tab.
3. Click on **Code Downloads & Errata**.
4. Enter the name of the book in the **Search** box and follow the onscreen instructions.

Once the file is downloaded, please make sure that you unzip or extract the folder using the latest version of:

- WinRAR/7-Zip for Windows
- Zipeg/iZip/UnRarX for Mac
- 7-Zip/PeaZip for Linux

The code bundle for the book is also hosted on GitHub at https://github.com/PacktPublishing/Machine-Learning-for-Data-Mining. In case there's an update to the code, it will be updated on the existing GitHub repository.

We also have other code bundles from our rich catalog of books and videos available at https://github.com/PacktPublishing/. Check them out!

Download the color images

We also provide a PDF file that has color images of the screenshots/diagrams used in this book. You can download it here:
`http://www.packtpub.com/sites/default/files/downloads/9781838828974_ColorImages.pdf`.

Conventions used

There are a number of text conventions used throughout this book.

`CodeInText`: Indicates code words in text, database table names, folder names, filenames, file extensions, pathnames, dummy URLs, user input, and Twitter handles. Here is an example: "Mount the downloaded `WebStorm-10*.dmg` disk image file as another disk in your system."

Bold: Indicates a new term, an important word, or words that you see onscreen. For example, words in menus or dialog boxes appear in the text like this. Here is an example: "Select **System info** from the **Administration** panel."

Warnings or important notes appear like this.

Tips and tricks appear like this.

Get in touch

Feedback from our readers is always welcome.

General feedback: If you have questions about any aspect of this book, mention the book title in the subject of your message and email us at `customercare@packtpub.com`.

Errata: Although we have taken every care to ensure the accuracy of our content, mistakes do happen. If you have found a mistake in this book, we would be grateful if you would report this to us. Please visit `www.packt.com/submit-errata`, selecting your book, clicking on the Errata Submission Form link, and entering the details.

Piracy: If you come across any illegal copies of our works in any form on the Internet, we would be grateful if you would provide us with the location address or website name. Please contact us at copyright@packt.com with a link to the material.

If you are interested in becoming an author: If there is a topic that you have expertise in and you are interested in either writing or contributing to a book, please visit authors.packtpub.com.

Reviews

Please leave a review. Once you have read and used this book, why not leave a review on the site that you purchased it from? Potential readers can then see and use your unbiased opinion to make purchase decisions, we at Packt can understand what you think about our products, and our authors can see your feedback on their book. Thank you!

For more information about Packt, please visit packt.com.

1
Introducing Machine Learning Predictive Models

A large percentage of data mining opportunities involve machine learning, and these opportunities often come with greater financial rewards. This chapter will give you the basic knowledge that you need to bring the power of machine learning into your data mining work. In this chapter, we're going to talk about the characteristics of machine learning models and also see some examples of these models.

The following are the topics that we will be covering in this chapter:

- Characteristics of machine learning predictive models
- Types of machine learning predictive models
- Working with neural networks
- A sample neural network model

Characteristics of machine learning predictive models

Knowing the characteristics of machine learning predictive models will help you understand the advantages and limitations in comparison to any statistical or decision tree models.

Let's get some insights on a few characteristics of predictive models in machine learning:

- **Optimized to learn complex patterns**: Machine learning models are designed to be optimized to learn complex patterns. In comparison to statistical models or decision tree models, predictive models greatly excel, when you have very complex patterns in data.

- **Account for interactions and nonlinear relationships**: Machine learning predictive models can account for interactions in the data and nonlinear relationships to an even better degree than decision tree models.
- **Few assumptions**: These models are powerful because they have very few assumptions. They can also be used with different types of data.
- **A black box model's interpretation is not straightforward**: Predictive models are black box models, this is one of the drawbacks of predictive machine learning models, because this implies that the interpretation is not straightforward. This means that, if we end up building many different equations and combine them, it becomes very difficult to see exactly how each one of these variables ended up interacting and impacting an output variable. So, the predictive machine learning models are great when it comes to predictive accuracy, but they're not that good for understanding the mechanics behind a prediction.

If you want to predict something, these models do a pretty good job and have amazing accuracy. But if you want to know why something is being predicted, and if you are looking forward to making some changes in the implementation so that you don't get a particular prediction, then it would be difficult to decipher.

Types of machine learning predictive models

The following are some of the different types of machine learning predictive models:

- Neural networks
- Support Vector Machines
- Random forest
- Naive Bayesian algorithms
- Gradient boosting algorithms
- K-nearest neighbors
- Self-learning response model

We won't be covering all of them, but we'll focus on a very interesting model – the neural network. In the following sections, we will get an in-depth view of what neural networks are.

Working with neural networks

Neural networks were initially developed in an attempt to understand how the brain operates. They were originally used in the areas of neuroscience and linguistics.

In these fields, researchers noticed that something happened in the environment (input), the individual processed the information (in the brain), and then reacted in some way (output).

So, the idea behind neural networks or neural nets is that they will serve as a brain, which is like a black box. We then have to try to figure out what is going on so that the findings can be applied.

Advantages of neural networks

The following are the advantages of using a neural network:

- **Good for many types of problems**: They work well with most of the complex problems that you might come across.
- **They generalize very well**: Accurate generalization is a very important feature.
- **They are very common**: Neural networks have become very common in today's world, and they are readily accepted and implemented for real-world problems.
- **A lot is known about them**: Owing to the popularity that neural networks have gained, there is a lot of research being done and implemented successfully in different areas, so there is a lot of information available on neural networks.
- **Works well with non-clustered data**: When you have non-clustered data, neural networks can be used in several situations, such as where the data itself is very complex, where you have many interactions, or where you have nonlinear relationships; neural networks are certainly very powerful and very robust solutions for such situations.

Disadvantages of neural networks

Good models come at the cost of a few disadvantages:

- **They take time to train**: Neural networks do take a long time to train; they are generally slower than a linear regression model or a decision tree model, as these basically just do one pass on the data, while, with neural networks, you actually go through many, many iterations.
- **The best solution is not guaranteed**: You're not guaranteed to find the best solution. This also means that, in addition to running a single neural network through many iterations, you'll also need to run it multiple times using different starting points so that you can try to get closer to the best solution.
- **Black boxes**: As we discussed earlier, it is hard to decipher what gave a certain output and how.

Representing the errors

While building our neural network, our actual goal is to build the best possible solution, and not to get stuck with a sub-optimal one. We'll need to run a neural network multiple times.

Consider this error graph as an example:

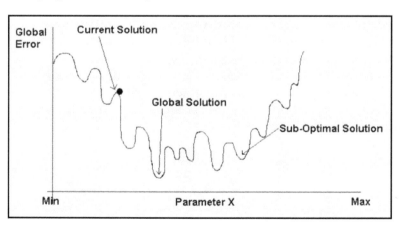

This is a graph depicting the amount of errors in different solutions. The **Global Solution** is the best possible solution and is really optimal. A **Sub-Optimal Solution** is a solution that terminates, gets stuck, and no longer improves, but it isn't really the best solution.

Types of neural network models

There are different types of neural networks available for us; in this section, we will gain insights into these.

Multi-layer perceptron

The most common type is called the **multi-layer perceptron model**. This neural network model consists of neurons represented by circles, as shown in the following diagram. These neurons are organized into layers:

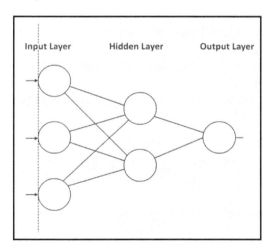

Every multi-layer perceptron model will have at least three layers:

- **Input Layer**: This layer consists of all the predictors in our data.
- **Output Layer**: This will consist of the outcome variable, which is also known as the **dependent variable** or **target variable**.
- **Hidden Layer**: This layer is where you maximize the power of a neural network. Non-linear relationships can also be created in this layer, and all the complex interactions are carried out here. You can have many such hidden layers.

You will also notice in the preceding diagram that every neuron in a layer is connected to every neuron in the next layer. This forms connections, and every connecting line will have a weight associated with it. These weights will form different equations in the model.

Why are weights important?

Weights are important for several reasons. First because all neurons in one layer are connected to every neuron in the next layer, this means that the layers are connected. It also means that a neural network model, unlike many other models, doesn't drop any predictors. So for example, you may start off with 20 predictors, and these 20 predictors will be kept. A second reason why weights are important is that they provide information on the impact or importance of each predictor to the prediction. As will be shown later, these weights start off randomly, however through multiple iterations, the weights are modified so as to provide meaningful information.

An example representation of a multilayer perceptron model

Here, we will look at an example of a multilayer perceptron model. We will try to predict a potential buyer of a particular item based on an individual's **age**, **income**, and **gender**.

Consider the following, for example:

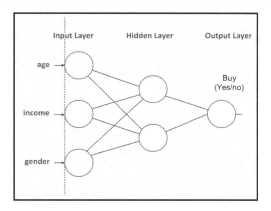

As you can see, our input predictors that form the **Input Layer** are **age**, **income**, and **gender**. The outcome variable that forms our **Output Layer** is **Buy**, which will determine whether someone bought a product or not. There is a hidden layer where the input predictors end up combining.

To better understand what goes on behind the scenes of a neural network model, lets take a look at a linear regression model.

The linear regression model

Let's understand the linear regression model with the help of an example.

Consider the following:

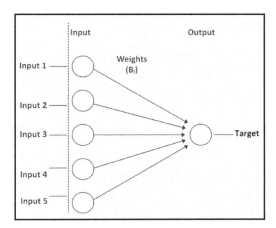

In linear regression, every input predictor in the **Input Layer** is connected to the outcome field by a single connection weight, also known as the **coefficient**, and these coefficients are estimated by a single pass through the data. The number of coefficients will be equal to the number of predictors. This means that every predictor will have a coefficient associated with it.

Every input predictor is directly connected to the **Target** with a particular coefficient as its weight. So, we can easily see the impact of a one unit change in the input predictor on the outcome variable or the **Target**. These kind of connections make it easy to determine the effect of each predictor on the Target variable as well as on the equation.

A sample neural network model

Let's use an example to understand neural networks in more detail:

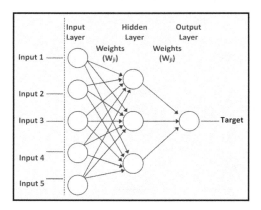

Notice that every neuron in the **Input Layer** is connected to every neuron in the **Hidden Layer**, for example, **Input 1** is connected to the first, second, and even the third neuron in the **Hidden Layer**. This implies that there will be three different weights, and these weights will be a part of three different equations.

This is what happens in this example:

- The **Hidden Layer** intervenes between the **Input Layer** and the **Output Layer**.
- The **Hidden Layer** allows for more complex models with nonlinear relationships.

- There are many equations, so the influence of a single predictor on the outcome variable occurs through a variety of paths.
- The interpretation of weights won't be straightforward.
- Weights correspond to the variable importance; they will initially be random, and then they will go through a bunch of different iterations and will be changed based on the feedback of the iterations. They will then have their real meaning of being associated with variable importance.

So, let's go ahead and see how these weights are determined and how we can form a functional neural network.

Feed-forward backpropagation

Feed-forward backpropagation is a method through which we can predict things such as weights, and ultimately the outcome of a neural network.

According to this method, the following iterations occur on predictions:

- If a prediction is correct, the weight associated with it is strengthened. Imagine the neural network saying, *Hey, you know what, we used the weight of 0.75 for the first part of this equation for the first predictor and we got the correct prediction; that's probably a good starting point.*
- Suppose the prediction is incorrect; the error is fed back or back propagated into the model so that the weights or weight coefficients are modified, as shown here:

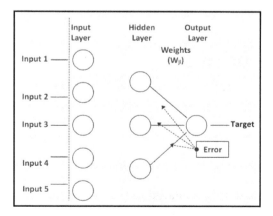

This backpropagation won't just take place in-between the **Hidden Layers** and the **Target** layer, but will also take place toward the **Input Layer**:

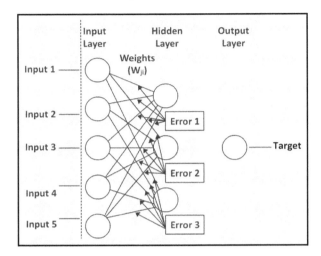

While these iterations are happening, we are actually making our neural network better and better with every error propagation. The connections now make a neural network capable of learning different patterns in the data.

So, unlike any linear regression or a decision tree model, a neural network tries to learn patterns in the data. If it's given enough time to learn those patterns, the neural network, combined with its experience, understands and predicts better, improving the rate of accuracy to a great extent.

Model training ethics

When you are training the neural network model, never train the model with the whole dataset. We need to hold back some data for testing purposes. This will allow us to test whether the neural network is able to apply what its learned from the training dataset to a new data.

We want the neural network to generalize well to new data and capture the generalities of different types of data, not just little nuances that would then make it sample-specific. Instead, we want the results to be translated to the new data as well. After the model has been trained, the new data can be predicted using the model's experience.

Summary

I hope you are now clear on machine learning predictive models and have understood the basic concepts. In this chapter, we have seen the characteristics of machine learning predictive models and have learned about some of the different types. These concepts are stepping stones to further chapters. We have also looked at an example of a basic neural network model. In the next chapter, we will implement a live neural network on a dataset and you will also be introduced to support vector machines and their implementation.

2
Getting Started with Machine Learning

In the last chapter, we saw what machine learning predictive models are and formed a basic understanding of how they work. In this chapter, we will demonstrate the working of neural net models and move on to another type of model, the (**Support Vector Machines**) **SVMs** model.

The following are the topics that will be covered in this chapter:

- Demonstrating a neural network
- Support Vector Machines
- Demonstrating SVMs

Demonstrating a neural network

Let's jump to a hands-on example of neural networks. The software that we are using is the SPSS Modeler, provided by IBM. But feel free to use any data-mining software package.

Running a neural network model

In order to run our first neural network, we will have to bring in the data that we will be using, if you are using IBM SPSS Modeler you can follow these steps:

1. Get the data using the **Var. File** node, and bring it up to the canvas:

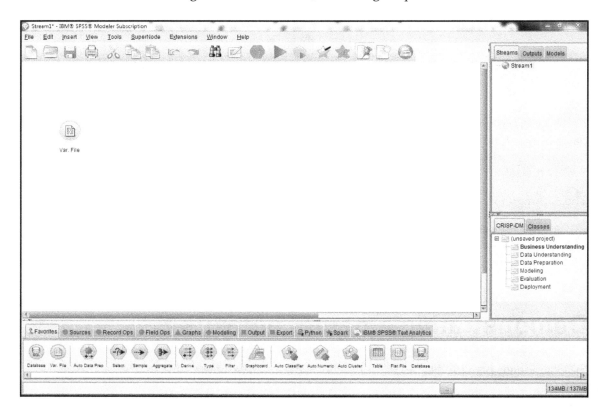

2. Attach the dataset to the source node:

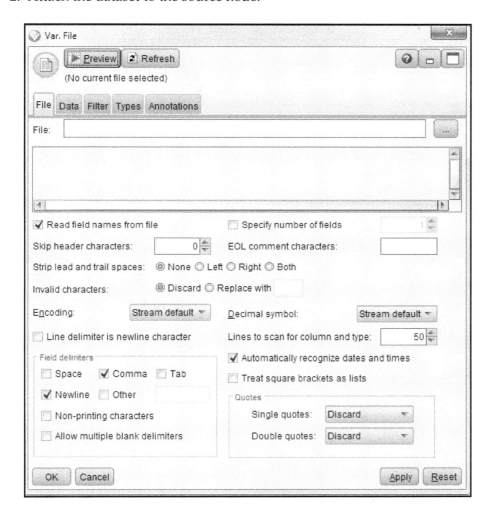

Click on the triple dot box on the right side of file box and navigate to your data; we are using `Electronics_Data` here:

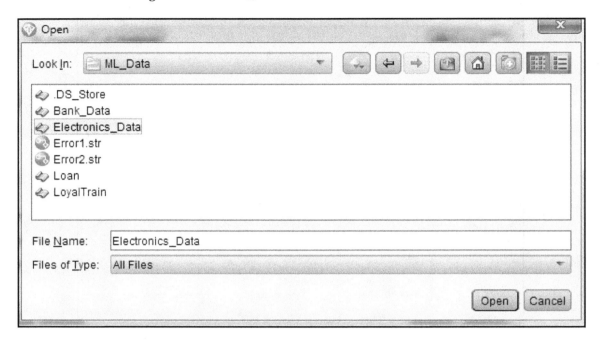

Click **Open**.

3. Go on to the **Types** tab to check whether the data was read correctly:

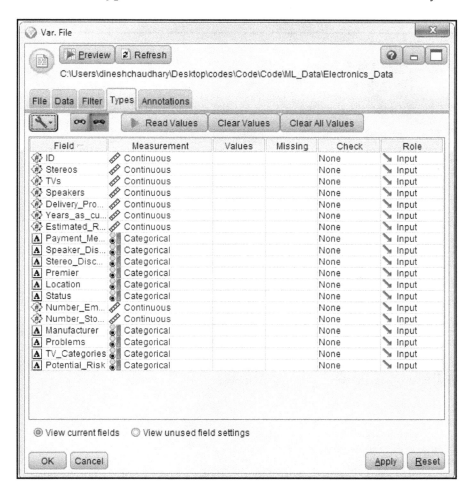

Click on the **Read Values** button; click **OK** on the prompt that pops up next, and you will see this:

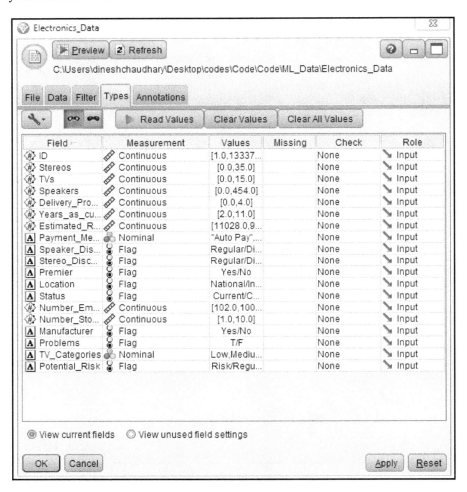

It looks like the data was read correctly.

4. We will not use the first variable, **ID**, and hence we will set its measurement to **Typeless**:

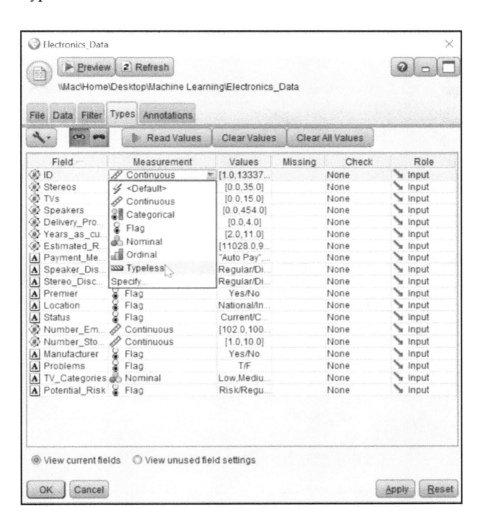

5. Let's now specify our **Status** target variable and set its **Role** to **Target**:

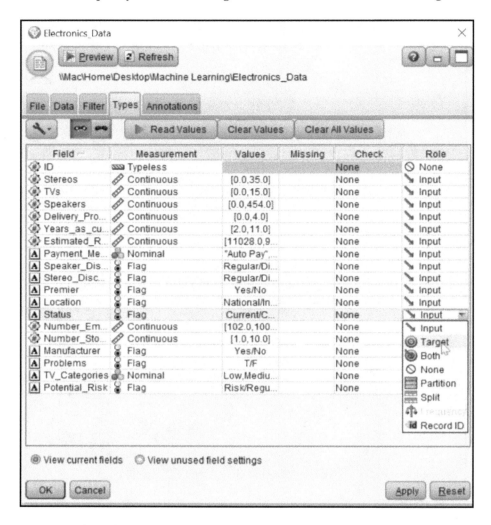

Now Modeler knows that the **Status** is the variable that it will be predicting. It will use the other fields to predict the outcome variable.

6. Take a look at the data that you have added; for this, go to the **Output** palette at the bottom of the canvas:

Connect the source node, `Electronics_Data`, to the Output Table node:

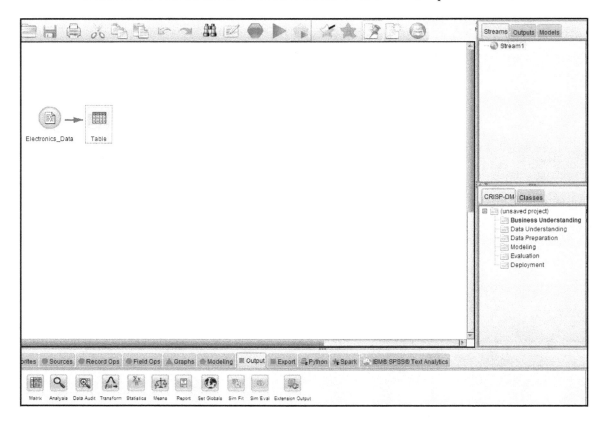

7. Run the stream by clicking the **Run Selection** (pentagon icon) button, beside the Play icon, located above the canvas:

You will see the following data:

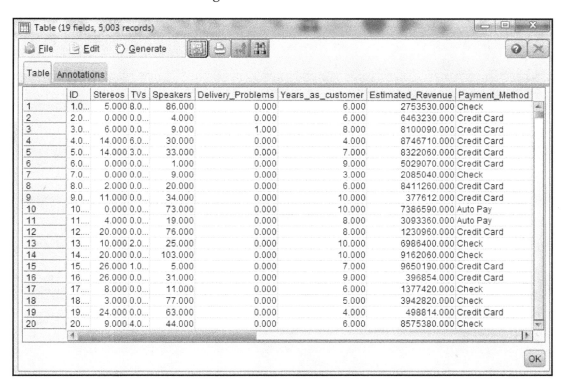

Hence, we have a table with **19 fields and 5,003 records**, and this means that we have 17 predictors in this dataset if we eliminate the target field and the ID field that we aren't using. We are going to predict the status field to check whether we have lost or retained a customer, based on the amount of items people have purchased, the total revenue, whether they have used discounts, the way in which they paid for the goods, the location, and other additional customer characteristics. Close this window to move ahead.

8. Before moving on to building any model, make sure to split your dataset into a `Training` and `Testing` dataset just to replicate your results and to verify the consistency in the model that we are building. For doing this, go to the **Field Ops** panel and connect the source node to the **Partition** node:

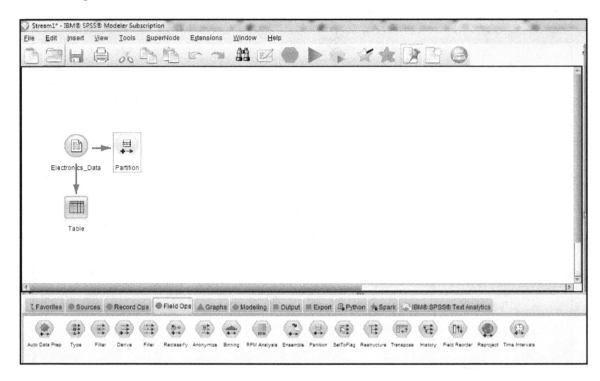

This **Partition** node will create two versions of the dataset:

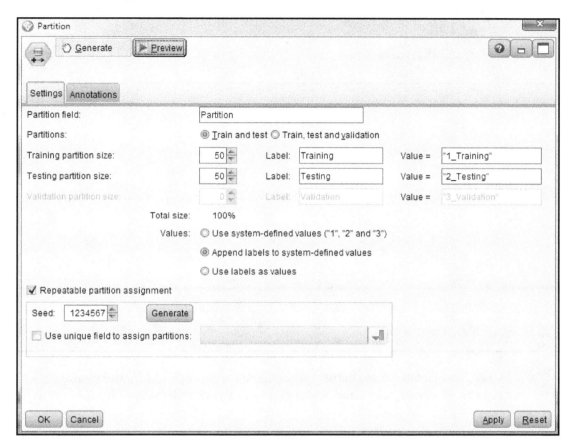

Hence, 50 of the data will be training and the other 50 of the dataset will be testing the dataset, respectively. Click **OK**.

9. We will now build our model. For this, go on to the **Modeling** panel and connect the **Partition** node to the **Neural Net** model by clicking once on both of them:

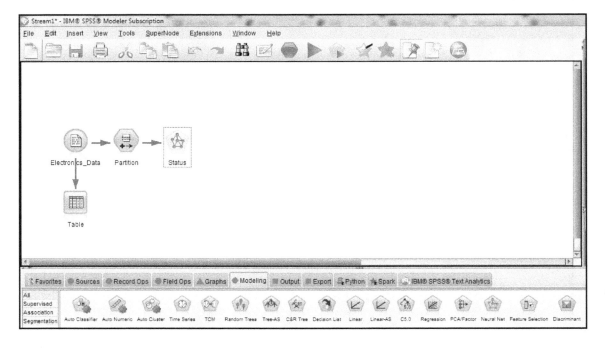

Hence, you can see that **Status**, the variable to be predicted by the neural network, is already captured and a neural network will be built for it.

10. Click on the **Neural Net** stat node to see the details of the neural network:

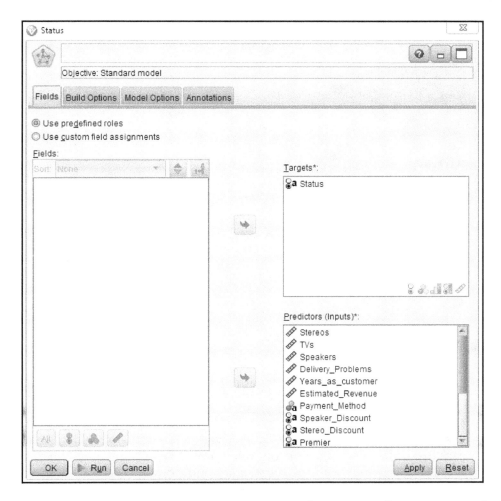

You can see that there is a target variable, and our 17 **Predictors** are specified by the neural network. The **Predictors** can be of any field type: continuous, categorical, or any other type. You can also decide to not include some of these **Predictors**.

11. Click on the **Build Options** tab:

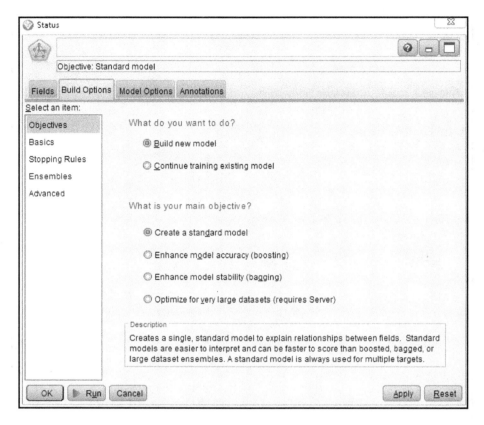

12. These questions are to know what you want to do with the model, whether you want to build a new model or continue training an existing one. You can select any objective here; we will be creating a standard model for our example, and we will discuss other options in later chapters.

13. You can see the type of model that you wish to build by clicking on the **Basics** tab under **Build Options**:

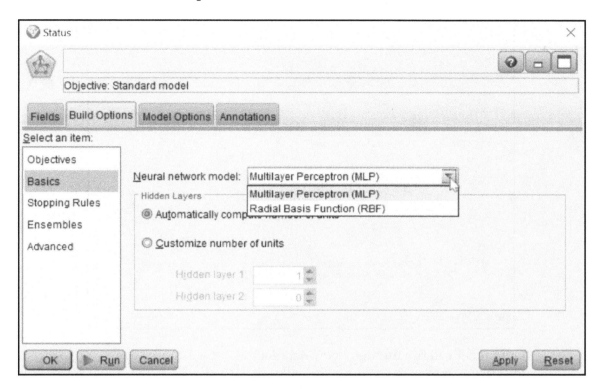

As you can see, we have two options, the **Multilayer Perceptron (MLP)** model, which we saw in this chapter earlier, and the **Radial Basis Function (RBF)** model. RBFs are preferred when you have things such as clustered predictors, but for our example the multilayer perceptron model is the best choice. The Hidden layers option allows you specify the number of Hidden layers you need in your model. Currently, we will select **Automatically compute number of units**. Hence, the model will automatically compute the number of hidden layers for us.

14. Go on to the **Shopping Rules** tab:

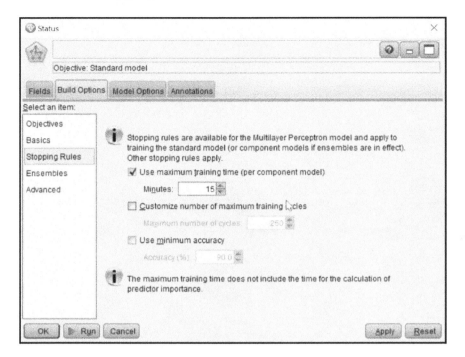

Our model will run through many iterations and it will stop when it's no longer improving; however, it can stop for other reasons as well. For example, it can stop after a certain amount of time has passed and the default, as you can see in the screenshot, is set to 15 minutes, but you can change this. You could also have the model stop after it's gone through a certain number of iterations, or you could tell the model to stop once it's reached a certain level of accuracy. Hence, these are some other ways in which you can stop running the model.

15. Click on the **Ensembles** tab:

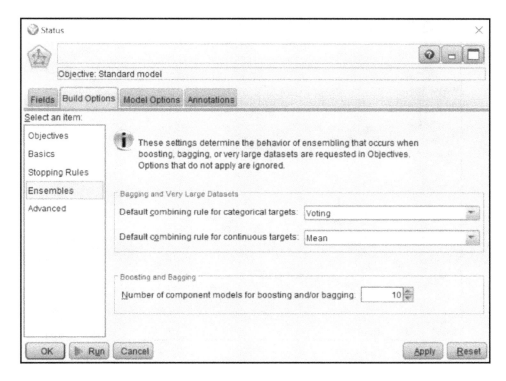

This option enables us to build multiple versions of a model; let's keep this at the default values.

16. Go on to the **Advanced** tab:

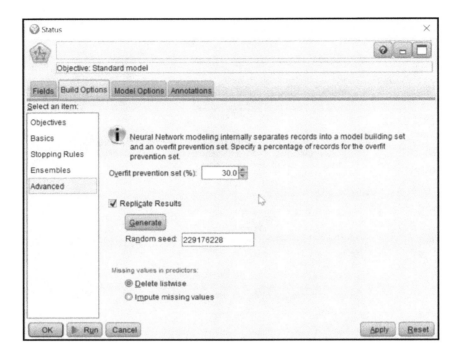

We know that neural nets will eventually learn the patterns in the data if you let them run for long enough. This can be an undesirable feature because we don't want to capitalize on chance, therefore we want hold some data back, and we can set the value of data to hold for each iteration using this option—in this case, of the training dataset is 30.0 is held back from the training dataset in every iteration.

Regarding the random seed, as we know, we will be running our model multiple times (the that we find the global solution and not get stuck on a sub-optimal solution), and we can generate the random seed. Each time you click on the Generate button, you will get a different random seed (or starting point).

Also, neural nets do not run with missing values; they need complete data, and you can select what needs to be done with the missing values using the **Advanced** tab **Missing values in Predictors** option:

- **Delete listwise**: If there is missing information on any one of the variables, that whole case will be eliminated from the model.
- **Impute missing values**: In this case, there are missing values, these will be replaced by the model defaults so you won't have any control over what Modeler does with them. Hence, my suggestion is to replace the missing values even before you start building a model.

17. Go to the **Model Options** tab:

The model is automatically going to give you or calculate the predictor importance. It'll let you know which fields are the most important in the model. In terms of what the model is going to provide, it's going to provide a prediction, and it's also going to provide a confidence in that prediction score. Typically, you should see the probability of a predicted value; that's the most useful.

You can also ask instead to get the increase in probability from the category that was predicted from the next-most-likely outcome. You can get predicted probabilities for the categorical targets for all the different categories if you like, as well.

The propensity scores end up being extremely useful, and we'll discuss them later.

18. Click on **Run** to run the model. Now the model has been built:

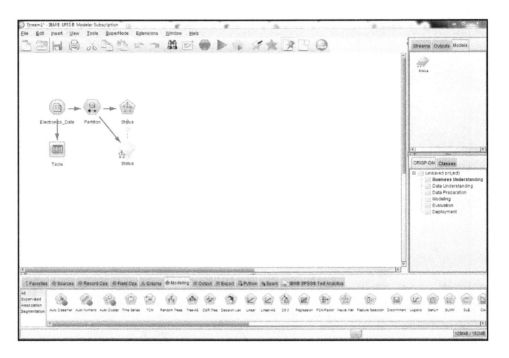

Let's see what we have found.

Interpreting results

To see the results, click on the **Status** generated model that was added automatically after the model was built.

The following observations are required for the testing dataset. Let's understand them in detail:

1. You will see a **Model Summary**:

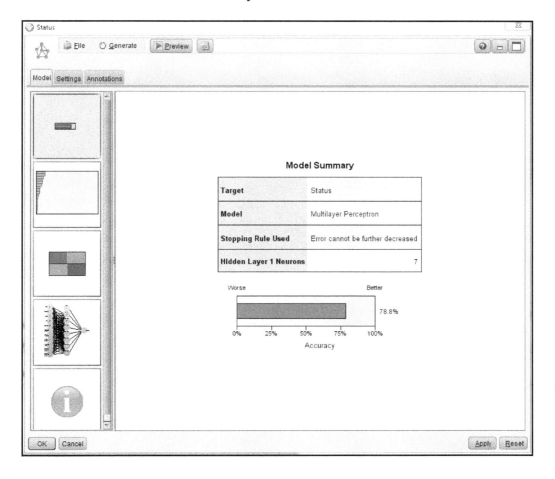

You can see what our target is; we know that we ran a multilayer perceptron model and then it gives you the information as to why the model stopped, and you can see that it stopped because the error cannot be further decreased. Basically, this means that the model was not improving anymore and we have one hidden layer and that hidden layer has seven neurons. We can also see that on the training dataset the overall accuracy was about **79%**.

2. Click on the next tab on the right side, the **Predictor Importance** tab:

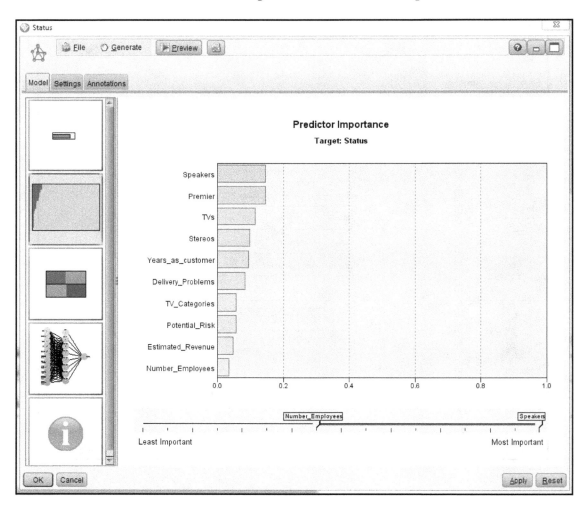

This gives you information on predictor importance. Hence, you can observe which predictors are the most important and contribute largely to the predictions. This is showing the most important predictors. In our case, the **Speakers** predictor tops the list. To see the importance of more predictors, you can just drag the scale down toward the left.

3. **Classification for Status** is our next observation:

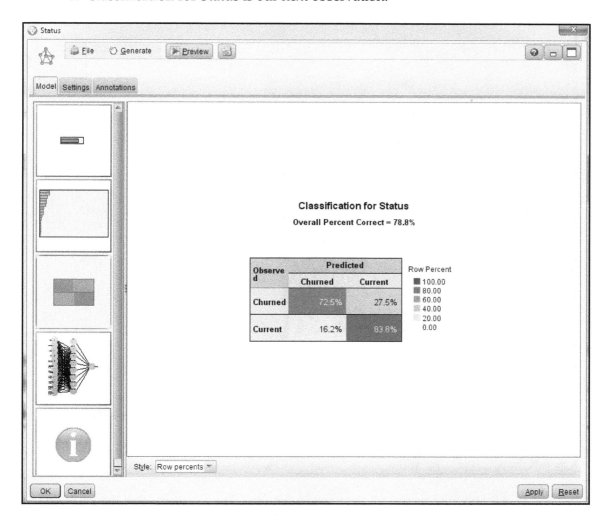

Here, we can see that how accurately we're predicting each one of the two groups in the training dataset; notice the overall percent correctly predicted. You can even switch to the cell-counts view form the **Style** tab at the bottom.

4. Let's go down a little further and click on the next tab:

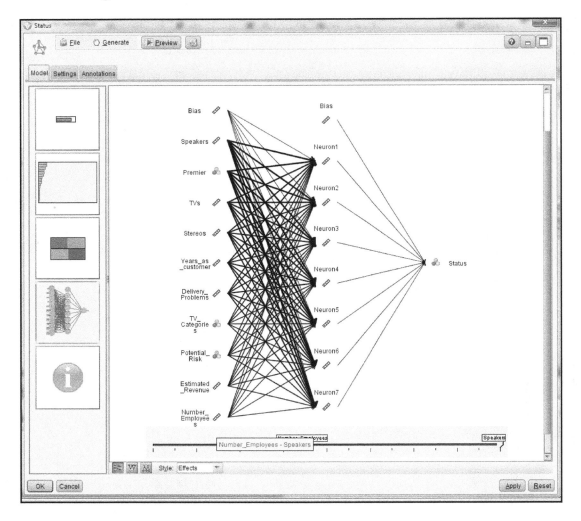

This is showing us the actual neural net model. We are predicting the variable status; we had one hidden layer, and that hidden layer had seven neurons, and this is what we can see here. You can see the connections from each one of the predictors to the neurons in the hidden layer.

You can also switch the **Style** from **Effects** to **Coefficients**:

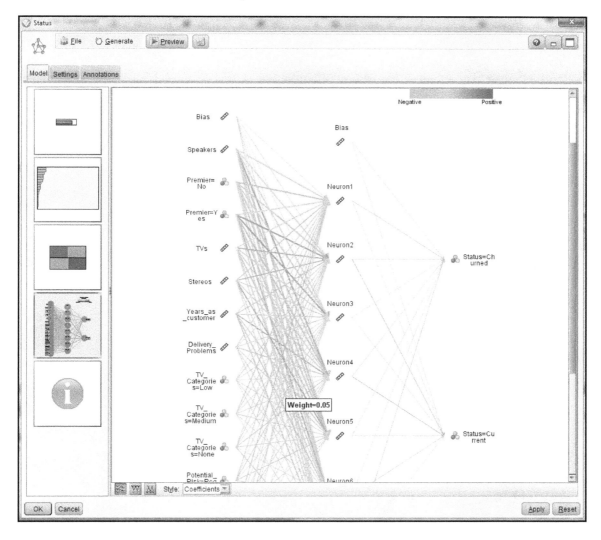

The thicker the line, the more important the predictor is in that equation, and you can even see the coefficients.

5. Click the final icon to get this information:

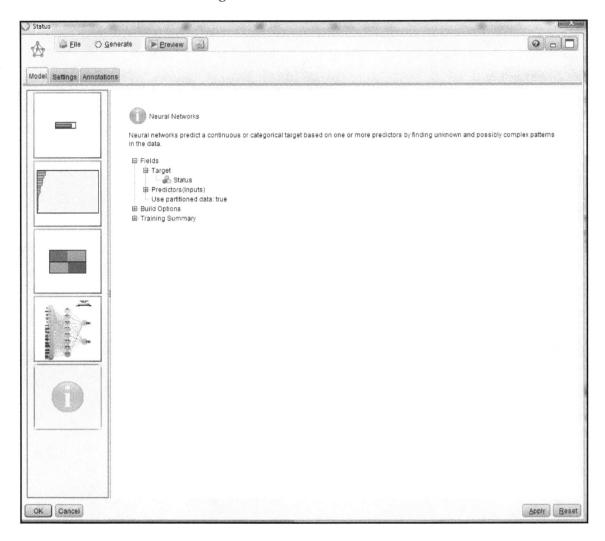

This just gives us information in terms of which field was our target and which ones are our predictors.

Close the window, and now we will see information about our training dataset. To do this, connect the model that we have to the **Table** icon:

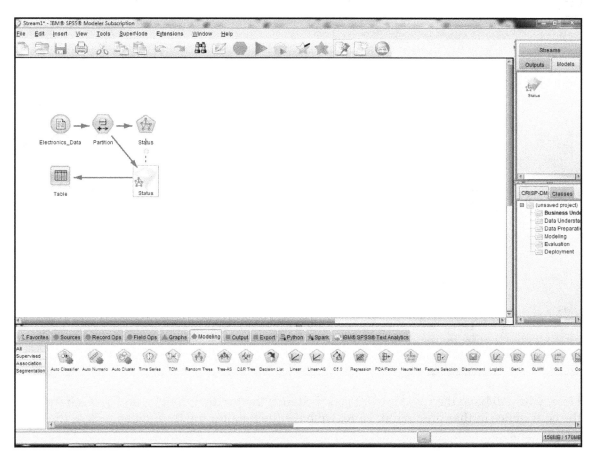

And you can run the Table node:

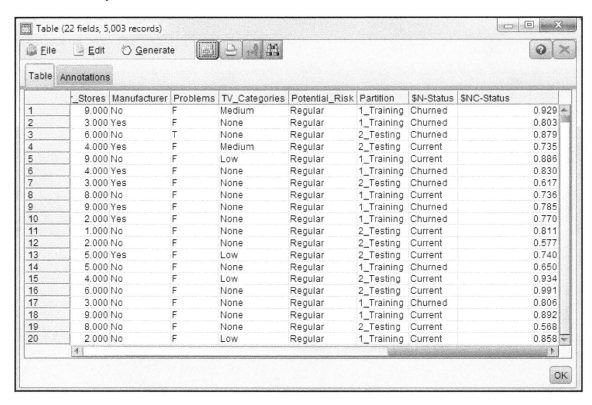

Here, you will have the two new fields, **$N-Status**, the prediction field, and **$NC-Status**, the confidence in that prediction. Here, we have the data for the training as well as the testing dataset.

Analyzing the accuracy of the model

Let's analyze the accuracy of the model:

1. In order to check the accuracy of the overall model, go to the **Output** palette and connect your model to the **Analysis** node:

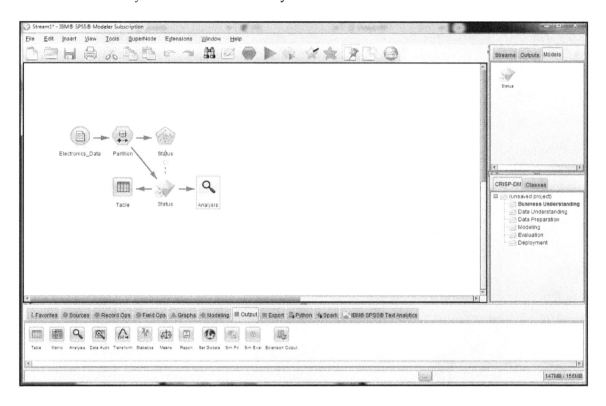

2. Click on the **Analysis** node and check the **Coincidence matrices (for symbolic targets)**:

The **Coincidence matrices (for symbolic targets)** is checked to give us additional information in terms of the breakdown of how accurate the model was.

3. On clicking **Run**, you can see the overall accuracy in the training and testing dataset:

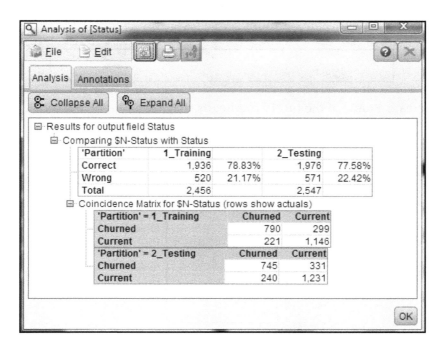

Remember we have seen the same accuracy result previously when we saw the model summary, around 79%. There is a slight drop in the accuracy of the testing dataset when compared to the training dataset, but it shouldn't matter much. The difference between the accuracy of both the datasets can be anywhere within 5% for the model to be reliable enough.

Hence, our training and testing data is pretty similar, and this means that we have built a consistent and reliable model that we can trust!

If you look at the **Confidence Matrix for $N-Status** part of the analysis, you can see that in the training dataset, we correctly predicted **790** people that are **Churned** and **1,146** people that are current customers. In the testing dataset, we correctly predicted **745** people who are **Churned**, and **1,231** people who are current customers.

Model performance on testing partition

Since we will running a Neural Net model multiple times, it is a good idea to create a couple of tables that show what was found:

Seed	Overall	Churned	Current	Consistent
229176228	77.58%	745 (68.4%)	1231 (83.7%)	Yes

You can also create a table of the top 10 predictors that are based on the seed that you used in the model:

229176228
Speakers
Premier
TVs
Stereos
Years as customer
Delivery problems
TV categories
Potential risk
Estimated revenue
Number employees

To evaluate the performance of your model, you can rerun the model in the same way as we have done until now multiple times and check the accuracy of the model each time you run it. You can even run it with a different seed and a different starting point. Therefore, the results obtained will be slightly different but fairly similar. As you know, we rerun the model multiple times to find the best possible solution.

To check the consistency in the results, you can keep expanding your model performance table in this manner each time you rerun the model:

Seed	Overall	Churned	Current	Consistent
229176228	77.58%	745 (68.4%)	1231 (83.7%)	Yes
641835376	78.17%	779 (71.5%)	1212 (82.4%)	Yes
1	79.7%	837 (76.9%)	1193 (81.1%)	Yes
2552	78.41%	787 (72.3%)	1210 (82.3%)	Yes
5000	80.29%	877 (80.5%)	1168 (79.4%)	Yes

Out of these models, you can choose the model that makes the most sense. For example, as you can see, the last entry with the seed of 5000 has the highest overall accuracy. It also has the highest number of accuracy in predicting churned customers. But it has the lowest accuracy in predicting the current customers. Hence, you can identify which solution is the most important for you and choose your best model accordingly.

The top 10 predictors for every rerun will also change with slight changes in the results. You can document the top 10 predictors each time you run the model and expand the top 10 predictors table that you created earlier:

229176228	641835376	1	2552	5000
Speakers	Premier	Premier	Premier	Premier
Premier	Speakers	Years as customer	Stereos	Years as customer
TVs	Years as customer	Speakers	Speakers	Stereos
Stereos	Stereos	TV categories	TVs	TVs
Years as customer	TVs	Stereos	Years as customer	Speakers
Delivery problems	Delivery problems	TVs	Delivery problems	TV categories
TV categories	Estimated revenue	Estimated revenue	Potential risk	Number employees
Potential risk	TV categories	Payment method	TV categories	Estimated revenue
Estimated revenue	Problems	Number employees	Estimated revenue	Delivery problems
Number employees	Number stores	Delivery problems	Number employees	Problems

As you can see, many predictors continue to be the most important, such as the premier predictor, whereas there are some predictors that appear only once or twice—for example, the **Number employees** predictor. These kinds of tables with a list of top 10 predictors can also help you to select the model that you need. You can also use this information to create a new version of a model where you don't want to use the predictors that you used initially but want to use only the predictors that either appear as the most common predictors in terms of the top ten or any predictor that appeared in the top ten.

Because we are already reducing the number of predictors, this would not only simplify the understanding of the model but also, ultimately, would end up creating a simpler model than in some cases, and this can actually be more accurate because you're getting rid of the extra noise that some of those other predictors might bring in.

Support Vector Machines

Support Vector Machines (**SVMs**) models were built to predict categorical and continuous outcomes and are especially good when you have many predictors. They were developed for difficult predicting situations where linear models were unable to separate the categories of the outcome field. They too work like black boxes, hiding their complex work in predicting results. Let's get an insight into how SVMs work.

Working with Support Vector Machines

Suppose, for example, there is a kind of data that cannot be separated using a single line as shown in this diagram:

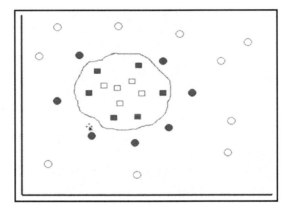

Consider these shapes to be different types of data. As you can see, we won't be able to separate a cluster of data by just drawing a single line between them. But the same job of differentiating can be done easily if a complex curve, such as a circle, is drawn instead of a line, just as in the diagram.

The main task of an SVM is to transform original data from this complex space to another space where the function that separates the data points is much simpler. This task is known as the **kernel transformation**.

Kernel transformation

The **kernel function** is a mathematical function that transforms the data. The reason why it's called an **SVM** is that the vectors form the boundaries between different groups of data, as shown in this diagram:

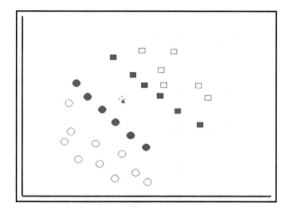

Hence, we have placed circles below and the squares above, and the boundaries are the vectors. These vector boundaries are separating the two groups. Vectors are the cases that act like boundaries between groups.

Hence, at this point, we can have several solutions:

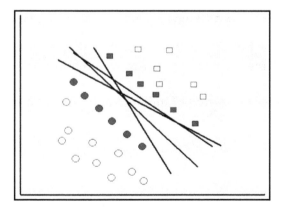

This shows that we no longer need a circle or complex curves to separate the groups of data.

But what is the best solution?

We ultimately need to find the best solution. The best solution will be the one that will maximize the separation between the groups while balancing the trade-off of potentially overfitting the function on new data. This new data includes a weight factor or a regularization factor that adds a penalty to the function to maximize the margin between the vectors while minimizing the error, as shown in the following diagram:

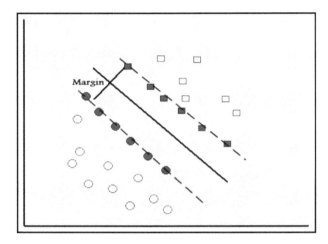

Types of kernel functions

In **SPSS Modeler**, there are four different types of kernel functions:

- **Linear**: A simple function that works well with few nonlinear relationships
- **Polynomial**: A more complex function that works well with some nonlinear relationships
- **RBF (Radial Basis Function)**: Similar to an RNN neural network that works well with nonlinear relationships
- **Sigmoid**: Similar to a two-layer neural network that works well with nonlinear relationships

Demonstrating SVMs

In this section, we will run an SVM model and see how it works.

First of all, get your dataset just the way you did for neural networks, partition the dataset into a training and testing dataset, and create a scenario such as this:

Let's see how to run SVMs:

1. Go to the **Modeling** palette and connect the partition node to **SVM**:

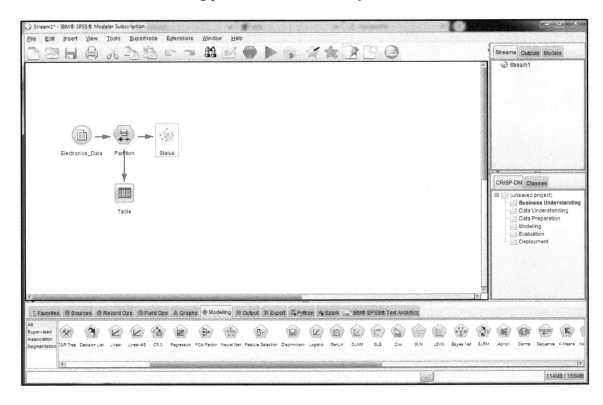

2. Go to the **Expert** tab and select the **Expert** option in **Mode**. Remember, whenever you run an **SVM** model, you must always run it in **Expert** mode because this is a model that requires constant changes on the default values based on the status of your model. The **Expert** mode will enable us to change the values easily when required:

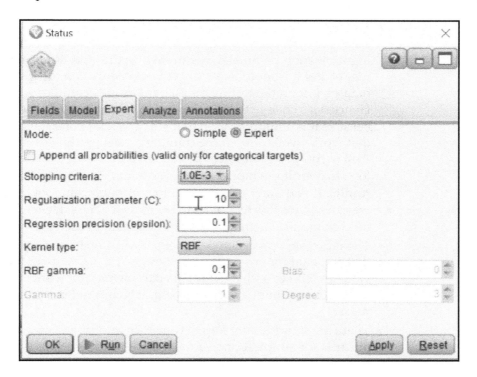

Let's discuss these options in detail:

- You can tick the **Append all probabilities** box when you have categorical outcomes. But, for now, let's keep it on default.
- The stopping criteria can also be changed, though you don't need to modify it that often.
- The regularization parameter is set to 10 by default, and you can select any values from 2 to 10. The higher the value of the regularization parameter, the more overfitting is done on your model and it is more likely to get better results on the training dataset, but on the testing dataset, the results could drop off. Hence, let's change the regularization parameter value to 5, because it is a middle value that will give us a consistent model that works well for both the training as well as the testing dataset. And if you get a consistent model at value 5, you can increase this to 7, to overfit the model just a little better, to get slightly better results. If you don't get consistent results at a value set to 5, then we can reduce this to 3 or so to try to overfit less. Hence, we will need to modify the regularization parameter based on our results.
- The regression precision parameter or epsilon is a pretty low value that is meant for errors. We want our errors to be lower than the value that is set in this field. This parameter only works when there is a continuous outcome field, which is not the case for our dataset.
- There are four types of kernel transformations that we have seen; linear is the simplest one, and we will start off with it. We can first test the model with a linear transformation, and if it does well, we can increase the complexity by selecting any other kind of transformation.

Here is a summary of the values that we have selected for the **Expert** tab:

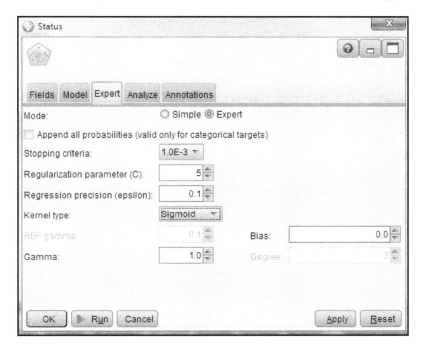

3. Click on the **Analyze** tab. Let's see what this tab includes:

   - We can calculate the propensity scores for this model; we will talk about this in later chapters.
   - The predictor importance can also be calculated. Here, for SVMs, this is not checked by default. The reason being that SVMs take a fairly long time to build the model if you select this option to calculate the predictor importance. You will run this model multiple times and change a lot of the parameters in the meantime. And finally when you find your best solution, or your ideal model, you will rerun the model, and that will be the time when you can check the option of calculating predictor importance. This will save a lot of time.

4. Click on **Run**. You will see a model built like this:

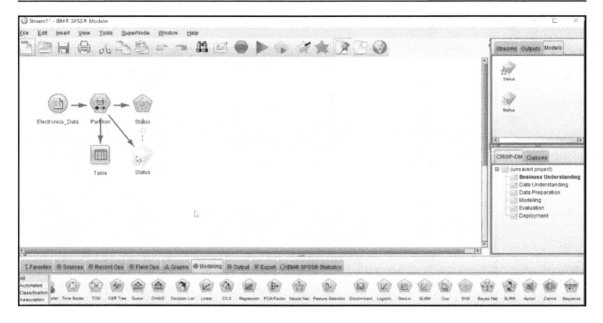

5. Now, connect the generated model to the table to see the results:

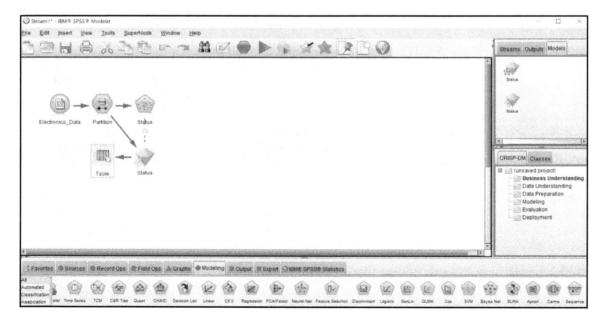

6. Click on **Table** and then click **Run**. If you scroll to the end, you will find predictions under **$S-Status** and **$SP-Status**:

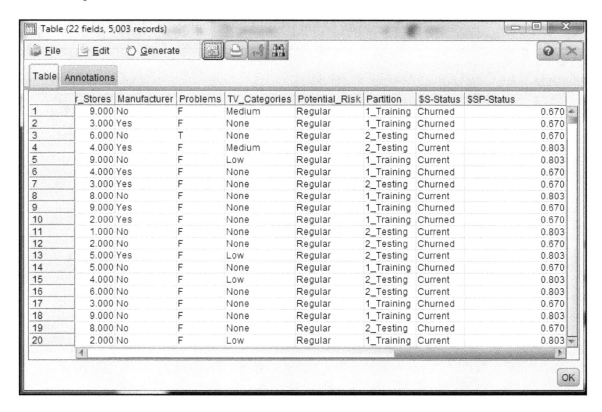

You can also see that we have got results for both the training and testing datasets, even though the model was built on the testing dataset.

7. You can now close the table's window, and click on the model, **Status**, to check the summary and model settings. Click on **OK**.

The model is currently like a black box. We don't know how we got the results and how it predicted the values. Let's find out.

Interpreting the results

Just as we did with the neural nets model, we will check the accuracy of the model that we have built. For this, select **Status** and go to the **Output** palette and select **Analyze**:

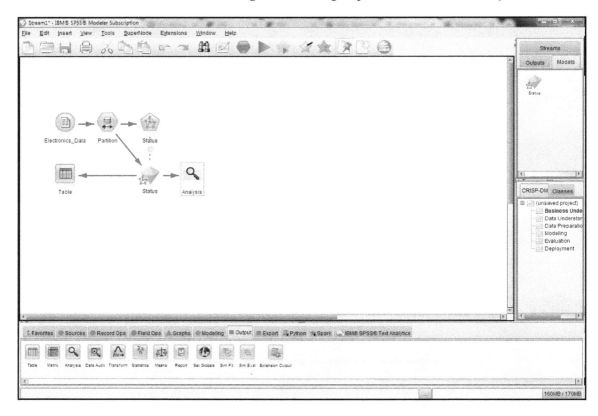

Click on **Analysis**, and as we have done before for the neural nets, click on **Coincidence matrices (for symbolic targets)** and click on **Run**; you will get this:

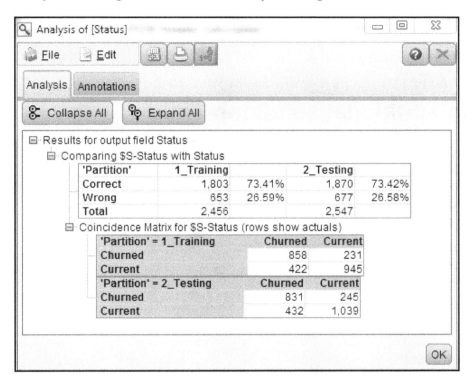

Hence, we have a very consistent model, currently!

Again, let's document the results in a table such as this one:

Model	Overall	Churned	Current	Consistent
Linear C=5	73.42%	831 (76.3%)	1039 (70.6%)	Yes

As you can see, in addition to the table made for neural nets, we have a type of model that we have used and even the regularization parameter value with which this was obtained. We have got a very consistent model, using the kernel transformation type as linear and the regularization parameter value set to **5**. But this also means that we can try with a slightly better value of the regularization parameter and see whether we can get a better solution. Let's move on to finding a better solution.

Trying additional solutions

Go back to the **SVM** model, **Status**, and click on the **Expert** tab. You can change the regularization parameter to something higher, as the model was consistent at 5; consider this an exercise. But, instead, we will change the **Kernel type** for our next run to the most complex **Sigmoid** type. It is not recommended to change the **Bias** value. But you can change **Gamma** for better results, and you can experiment on those values later. For now, we will keep them on default, and click on **Run**:

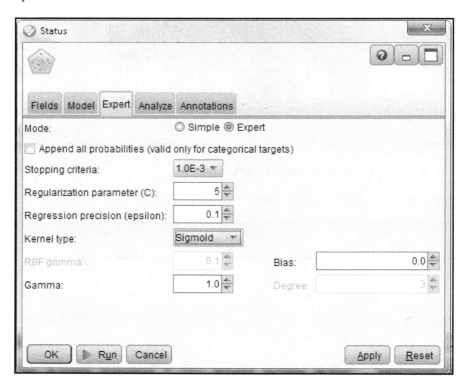

Click on the **Analyze** tab, and then click on **Run**. Here is our result:

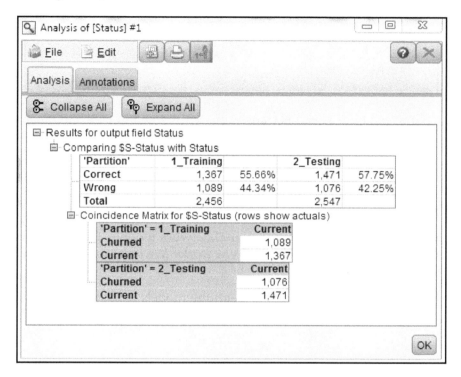

The model is consistent, but as you can see, the accuracy percentage is significantly lower than what we found in our linear model. Hence, this model has not done a better job compared to what the linear model did. This means that the Sigmoid type didn't work well.

This brings us to the conclusion that the best type of kernel transformation suited for our dataset is the most simple, linear transformation. Because the data is also not really that complex either. But, you must rerun the model multiple times to verify your results.

Here is my analysis from the models that I ran:

Model	Overall	Churned	Current	Consistent
Linear C=5	73.42%	831 (76.3%)	1039 (70.6%)	Yes
Polynomial C=5; Degree = 2	80.17%	820 (75.3%)	1222 (83.1%)	Yes
RBF C=5; RBF gamma = .27	79.94%	842 (77.3%)	1194 (81.2%)	No
Sigmoid C=5; Gamma = 1	57.75%	0 (0%)	1471 (100%)	Yes

You can now see which type of kernel transformation worked in which manner with each of the predictors. You can select predictors that are important to you and select that as the best model.

Summary

In this chapter, we saw how to work with neural network models. Then we moved on to cover SVM models and demonstrated how SVM works. We have seen how to work with different types of kernel transformations.

In the next chapter, we will look at machine learning models in more detail.

3
Understanding Models

In this chapter, we're going to look into general model interpretation. We will have a look at the different types of predictive models. Then we will interpret some machine learning models using various techniques.

We will be covering the following topics in this chapter:

- Types of models
- Using graphs to interpret machine learning models
- Using statistics to interpret machine learning models
- Using decision trees to interpret machine learning models

Models

There are three different types of predictive models:

- Statistical models
- Decision tree models
- Machine learning models

Statistical models

The first thing that the statistical models identify is which predictors are most important in a model. The statistical models also create an equation that allows you to make predictions. For example, as we can see in the following screenshot, the coefficients that are part of the prediction equation have been highlighted:

		Coefficients				
		Unstandardized Coefficients		Standardized Coefficients		
Model		B	Std. Error	Beta	t	Sig.
1	(Constant)	135.904	983.582		.138	.890
	salbeg	1.734	.059	.799	29.331	.000
	edlevel	298.049	67.220	.126	4.434	.000
	age	-58.950	12.734	-.102	-4.629	.000

Linear Regression Formula:

$$Y = a + b_1x_1 + b_2x_2 + ... + b_ix_i$$

Current Salary = 135.9 + 1.7(Beginning Salary) + 298 (Education Level) − 59 (Age)

The following screenshot highlights the equation to predict current salaries:

Coefficients					
		Unstandardized Coefficients		Standardized Coefficients	
Model		B	Std. Error	Beta	t	Sig.
1	(Constant)	135.904	983.582		.138	.890
	salbeg	1.734	.059	.799	29.331	.000
	edlevel	298.049	67.220	.126	4.434	.000
	age	-58.950	12.734	-.102	-4.629	.000

Linear Regression Formula:

$$Y = a + b_1x_1 + b_2x_2 + ... + b_ix_i$$

Current Salary = 135.9 + 1.7(Beginning Salary) + 298 (Education Level) − 59 (Age)

In the following screenshot, we can see that we take the coefficient for the variable beginning salary and we multiply it by the actual beginning salary:

Coefficients					
		Unstandardized Coefficients		Standardized Coefficients	
Model		B	Std. Error	Beta	t	Sig.
1	(Constant)	135.904	983.582		.138	.890
	salbeg	1.734	.059	.799	29.331	.000
	edlevel	298.049	67.220	.126	4.434	.000
	age	-58.950	12.734	-.102	-4.629	.000

Linear Regression Formula:

$$Y = a + b_1x_1 + b_2x_2 + ... + b_ix_i$$

Current Salary = 135.9 + 1.7(Beginning Salary) + 298 (Education Level) − 59 (Age)

Now, we take the coefficient for education level and we multiply it by a person's number of years of education:

	Coefficients					
		Unstandardized Coefficients		Standardized Coefficients		
Model		B	Std. Error	Beta	t	Sig.
1	(Constant)	135.904	983.582		.138	.890
	salbeg	1.734	.059	.799	29.331	.000
	edlevel	298.049	67.220	.126	4.434	.000
	age	-58.950	12.734	-.102	-4.629	.000

Linear Regression Formula:

$$Y = a + b_1x_1 + b_2x_2 + \ldots + b_ix_i$$

Current Salary = 135.9 + 1.7(Beginning Salary) + 298 (Education Level) − 59 (Age)

We also need the person's **age**, which is highlighted in the following screenshot:

	Coefficients					
		Unstandardized Coefficients		Standardized Coefficients		
Model		B	Std. Error	Beta	t	Sig.
1	(Constant)	135.904	983.582		.138	.890
	salbeg	1.734	.059	.799	29.331	.000
	edlevel	298.049	67.220	.126	4.434	.000
	age	-58.950	12.734	-.102	-4.629	.000

Linear Regression Formula:

$$Y = a + b_1x_1 + b_2x_2 + \ldots + b_ix_i$$

Current Salary = 135.9 + 1.7(Beginning Salary) + 298 (Education Level) − 59 (Age)

We multiply all the values with their respective coefficients, and finally, we add all the constants, which predicts what the person's salary is going to be. Now that's great. But in addition, the statistical models allow us to determine the effect of a one-unit increase in each predictor, and you can see the effect of this predictor on the different outcome variables.

So, for example, with education level, we see that it has a coefficient of **298**. That tells us that a person's current salary is increasing by $298 for each additional year of education that the person has:

	Coefficients					
		Unstandardized Coefficients		Standardized Coefficients		
Model		B	Std. Error	Beta	t	Sig.
1	(Constant)	135.904	983.582		.138	.890
	salbeg	1.734	.059	.799	29.331	.000
	edlevel	298.049	67.220	.126	4.434	.000
	age	-58.950	12.734	-.102	-4.629	.000

Linear Regression Formula:

$$Y = a + b_1x_1 + b_2x_2 + ... + b_ix_i$$

Current Salary = 135.9 + 1.7(Beginning Salary) + 298 (Education Level) − 59 (Age)

So you can really see the impact of each individual independent variable and how it ends up impacting the overall prediction.

Decision tree models

Just like statistical models, decision tree models help you identify which predictors are most important in the model. There are no equations, and we can't determine a one-unit impact and along with the effect that it has on an outcome variable. Instead we are going to create rules that make predictions by segmenting data in two mutually-exclusive categories.

So, for example, as you can see in the following screenshot, we have anybody with a variable **Premier** value of **No**:

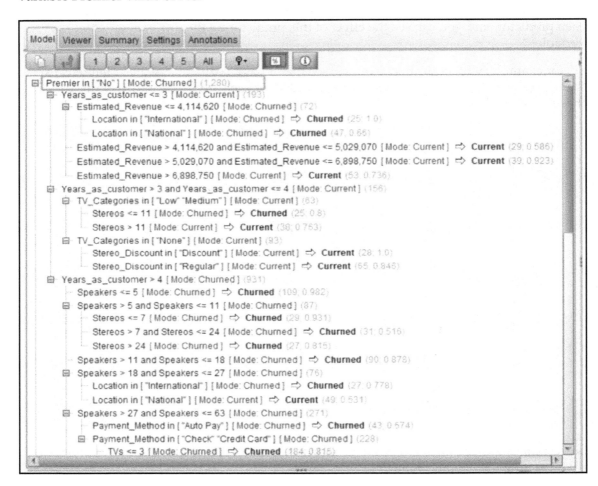

We have anybody that was a customer for three years or fewer, as shown in the following screenshot:

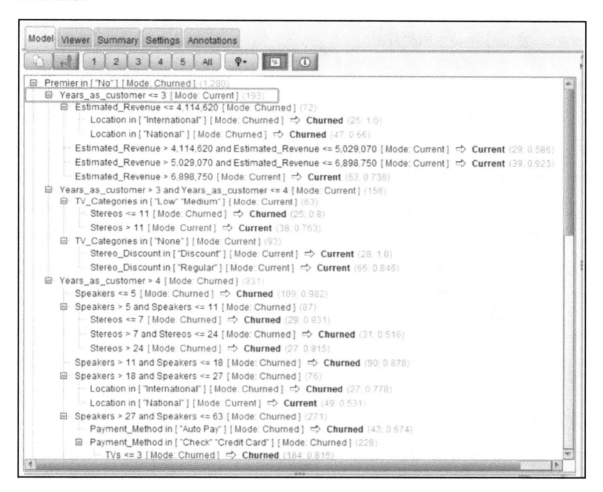

And we have people whose estimated revenue was less than or equal to about 4,000,000, as shown in the following screenshot:

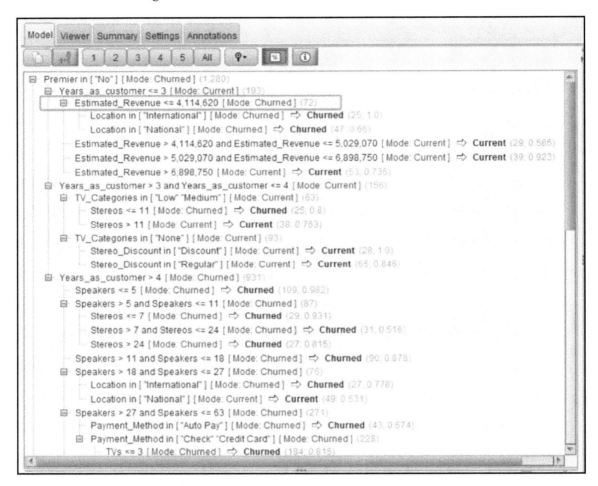

They happen to be located in another country, and we're predicting that they're going to churn, as shown in the following screenshot:

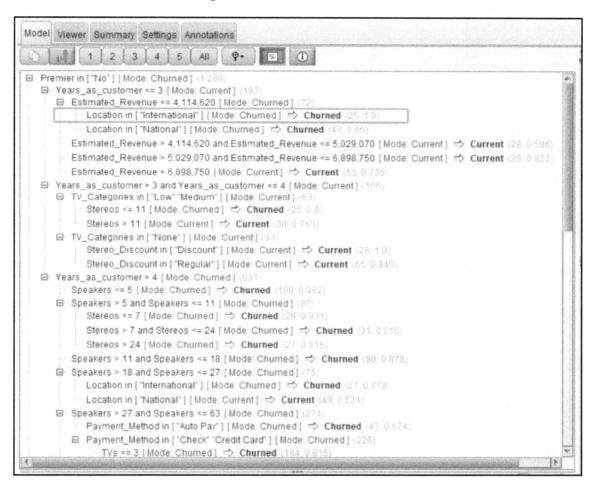

This rule was applied to 25 people, and the accuracy of that rule was 100%, as shown in the following screenshot. So, for all the customers who fit those criteria, we ended up losing them as customers 100% of the time.

Next, there's a second rule, and it's exactly the same as the first. The only difference is that the location is a **National** customer, and you will notice that we're still predicting the people who will be churned. That rule applies to **47** individuals, but the accuracy of that rule is only 66%:

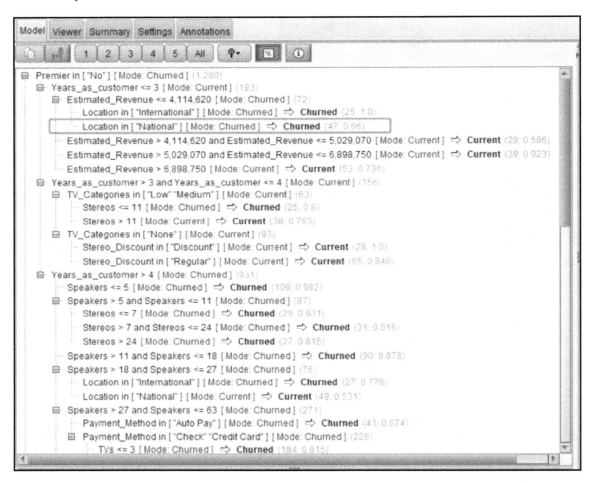

Now, at first glance it might seem that these are fairly similar rules, but this is where you have to go back and try to identify what's really going on.

Notice that when all the criteria were met and we happen to have an international customer, we always lost them, but when we have a **National** customer, we still are most likely to lose them, but we didn't lose all of them. You might want to ask yourself why? Well, maybe you could go back over to the sales reps. They might inform you that they call the **National** customers once a quarter just to see how they're doing and that one call manages to keep some of those customers, so that you don't end up losing them. So, Decision trees allow you to create these different rules that allow you to make predictions, and then you can see the inner workings of the model very well.

Machine learning models

Like both statistical and decision tree models, machine learning models identify which predictors are the most important in the model.

In the following example of a neural net model, we see that the **Speakers** variable was the most important, followed by **Premier**, followed by **TVs**:

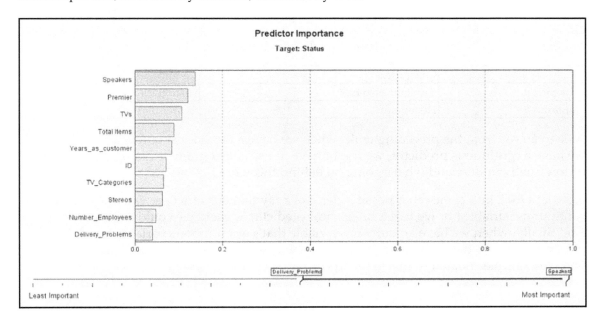

So, those are the most important predictors and that's all we get. We don't get any equations or a rule. We don't even know the direction of the relationship, for example, are we more likely to keep or lose customers that buy more speakers? We really don't know; we don't get that kind of information from any machine learning model because they're all black boxes.

Hence, in the next section, we're going to see how you would figure out exactly how to interpret the results of a machine learning model. Also, we'll see how to use graphs to interpret machine learning models.

Using graphs to interpret machine learning models

In this section, we're going to see how to use graphs to interpret the results of a machine learning model. Specifically, it's important to know what kind of data you have, because the type of data will determine the type of graph that you can create. This graph will then help you understand what goes into the predictions of a machine learning model. We will also understand how a machine learning model uses these different variables for the predictions and eventually use these predictions for our final interpretation.

For example, when we have an outcome variable that is a categorical variable and our predictor is also a categorical variable, we can use a bar chart or a web plot. We can use either type of graph to help us understand how the machine learning model is making its predictions. The following table represents data and graph combinations:

	Categorical	Continuous
Categorical	Bar chart/web plot	Histogram
Continuous	Histogram	Scatter plot

As we can see from the preceding table, when we have a categorical outcome variable but we have a continuous predictor, we might have to use a histogram. A histogram can help us to visually understand what's going on behind those predictions.

Now let's look into some other possibilities. Let's say that our outcome variable is actually a continuous variable but we had a categorical predictor, so here we could use a histogram. And finally, when we have an outcome variable that's a continuous variable and a predictor variable that's also a continuous variable, we can end up using a scatter plot. We will see examples related to this in the upcoming sections.

In the previous section, we built a neural net model. Let's take a look at the model that we built:

1. Let's use the model that we created in the previous chapter:

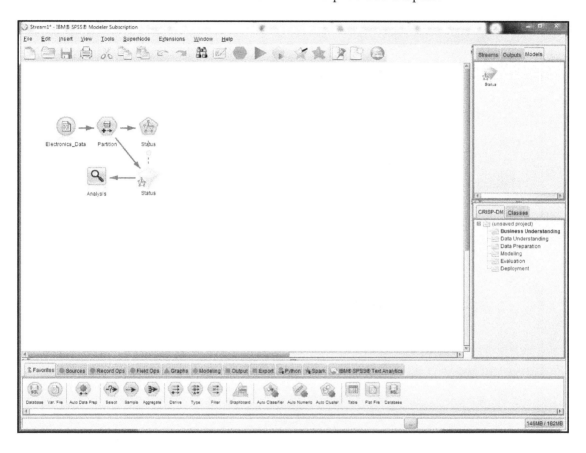

2. Set the **Random seed** as 5000 and then run the model

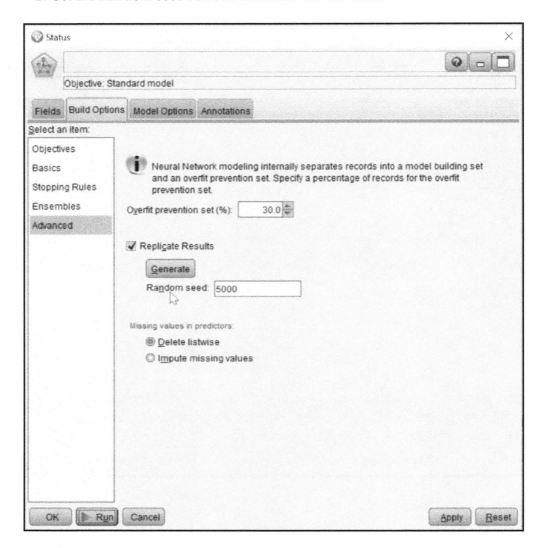

3. Click on the newly generated model and in the observations, we can see that the **Premier** variable is the most important predictor, followed by **Years_as_customer**, and then **Stereos**, **TVs**, and so forth:

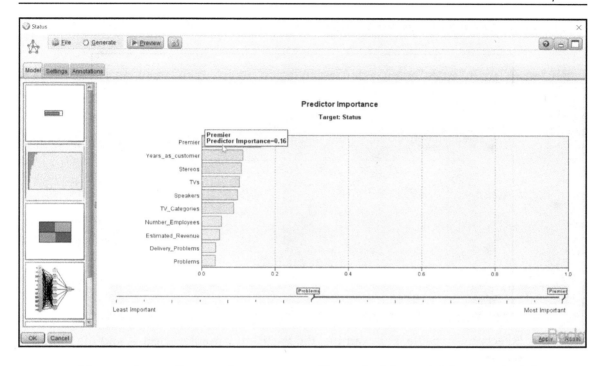

Now we know the most important predictors in this model, but we don't know how these predictors are being used by the model. Therefore, we will investigate their relationships.

There are several ways in which we can know about the relationships between components of the model. We can use graphs or tables. Let's go through a few examples:

4. Select the **Record Ops** palette.
5. Connect the generated model over to a **Select** node.
6. Let's look at the data for the training dataset. We will keep the testing dataset separate because we will use that data later to confirm the findings.
7. Click on the **Select** node to edit it.

8. Click on the **Expression Builder**:

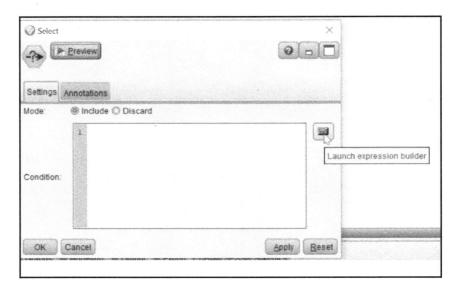

9. Select any variable. For example, the **Partition** variable, select =, and the training dataset:

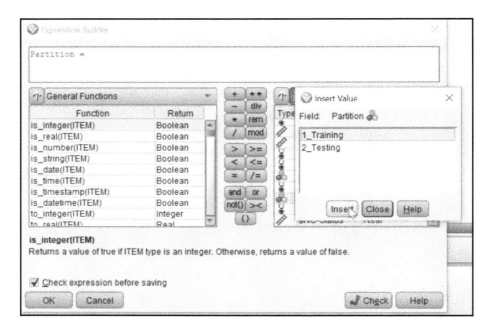

10. This is how a expression will look also, click on **OK**:

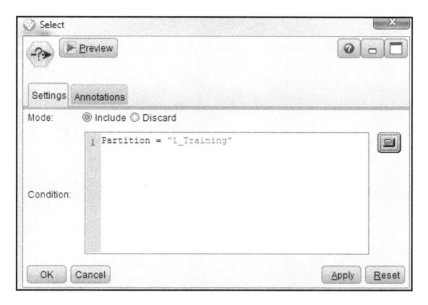

We have selected only the people in the training dataset. Now, let's take a look at the relationships between the actual predictions and the important variables in this model to figure out exactly how these variables are used by the model:

11. Go to the **Graphs** palette and connect the **Select** node to a **Distribution** node. The **Distribution** node is basically a bar chart, as shown in the following screenshot:

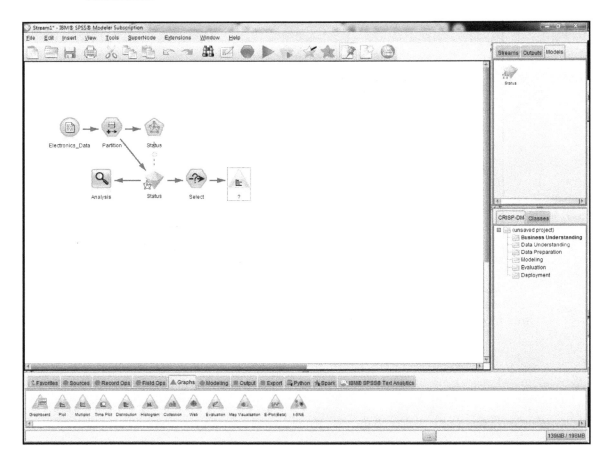

12. Edit the **Distribution** node. Select the **Premier** field:

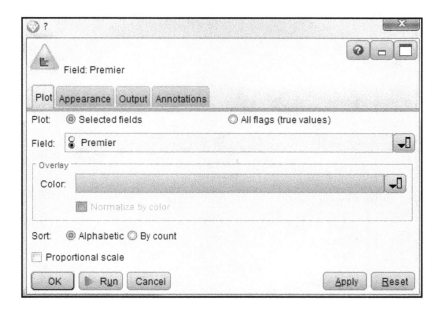

Notice that only categorical fields are available here:

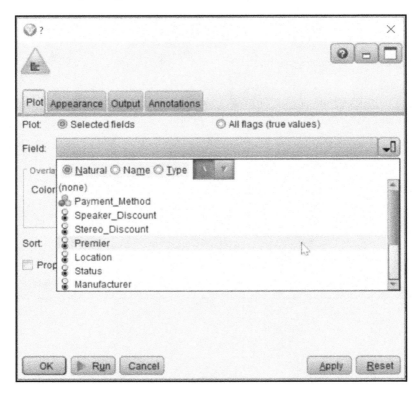

We are selecting the **Premier** variable because that was the most important predictor in the model and we will see how that variable is used in its predictions:

13. Click on the overlay button:

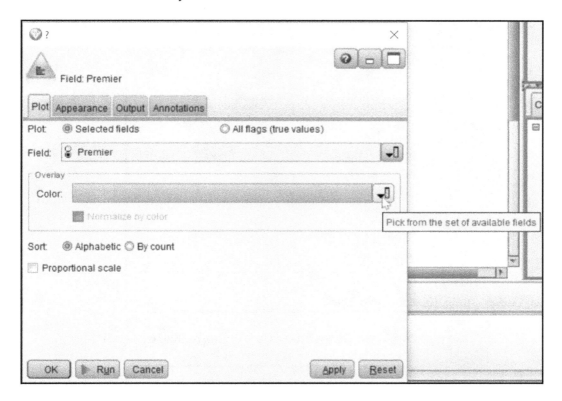

14. Select the variable **$N-Status**, which is our actual prediction:

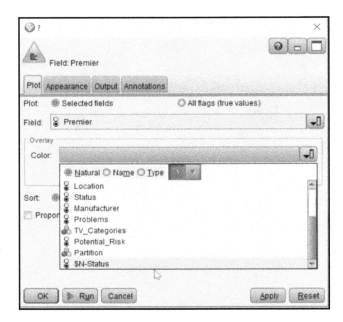

15. To make comparisons a little easier, click on normalize by **Color**:

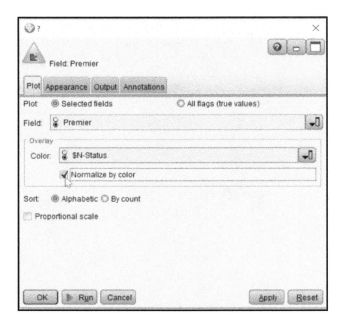

16. Click on **Run** and you can see what was done here:

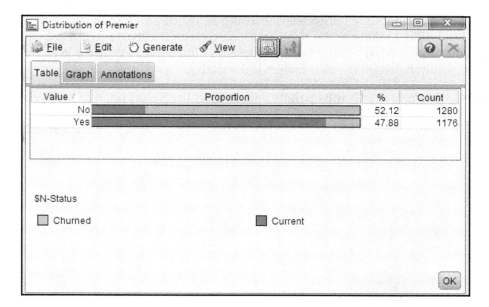

Notice that the blue color is associated with those who were predicted as going to churn, and the red color is associated with people who were predicted as current customers. You can also see that the people that are **Premier** customers we are associating them with being a current customer. The people that are not **Premier** customers we are associating them with the blue color which means that we're predicting that they're going to churn.

So that's how you investigate the relationship between a categorical predictor and a categorical outcome variable. We could use something similar to a bar chart, in this case, it's called the **Distribution** node in Modeler; it would be called as a **bar chart** in other software packages, but you're looking at the relationship between these two categorical variables and now you can see what's going on with these relationships. Let's use a **Web** node to look at the relationship between the two categorical variables:

1. Go down to the **Graphs** palette and connect the **Select** node to the **Web** node:

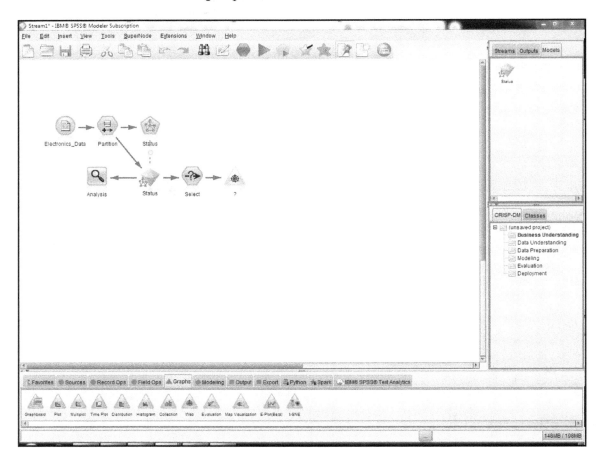

2. Edit the **Web** node, you can either build this as a **Web**, which basically allows us to take a lot of categorical variables and put them all together, or we can create a **Directed web** so that all the categorical variables in those categories are all directed towards one specific variable, which is what we are going to do here. Choose the **Directed web**.

3. Click on the field box

4. Add your prediction, which is the **$N-Status** variable, add all other categorical variables:

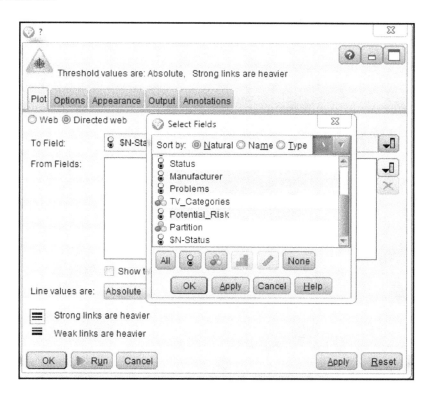

5. The following screenshot shows all the selected flag fields:

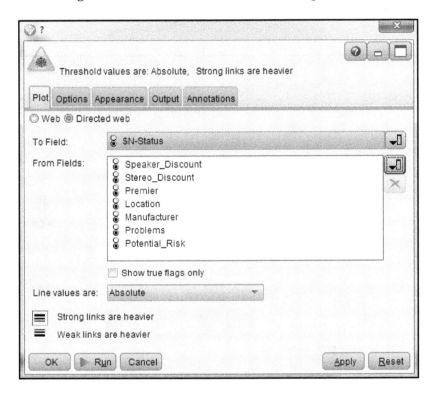

6. Add other categorical fields. Select **Payment_Method**:

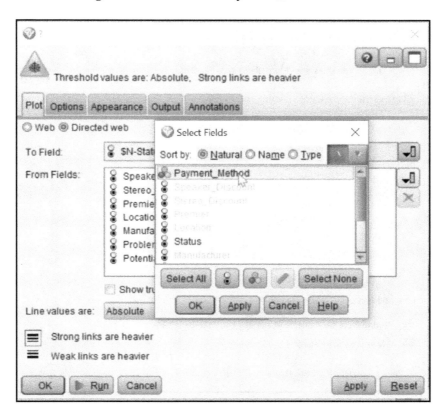

7. Hold the *Ctrl* key and scroll down and select **TV_Categories** and click on **OK**:

8. Set the **Line values** to **Absolute**, as shown in the following screenshot:

9. Set **Line values are** to **Percentages of "From" the field/value**. From these **Predictor** fields, we will see how these values are related to the **Outcome** field and click on Run:

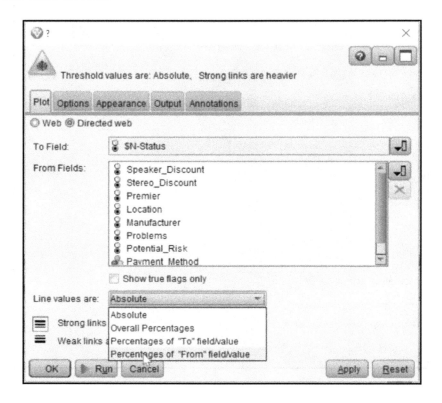

Notice that there are two lines that are a little thicker than the others:

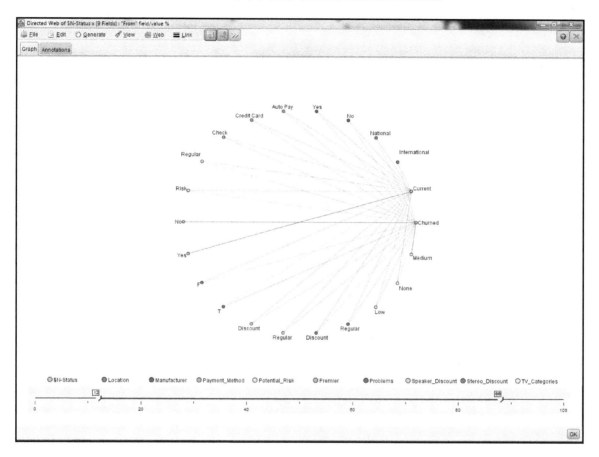

You can see that one of the line values says **Yes**. The other line value says **No** and they're both related to the field current and churned as we can see in the following output

Let's take a look at the thickest **Yes** line:

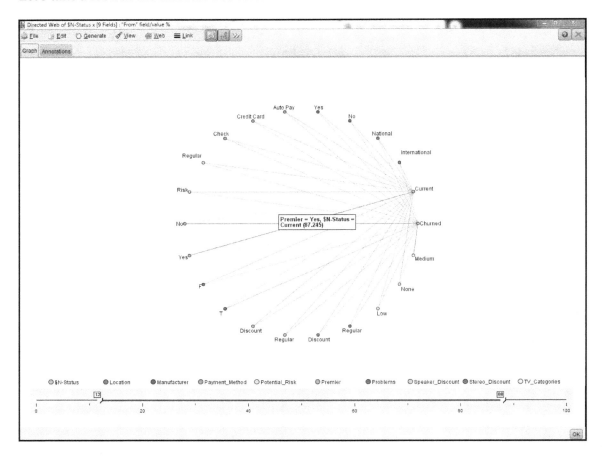

We can see that this line is showing us that these are people that on the **Premier** variable had a value of **Yes** and the prediction is associated with being a current customer and then we can see that **87%** of the people that are predicted to be current customers they had a value of **Yes** on the variable **Premier**.

Similarly, the next thickest line would be the one where we're on the **Premier** variable. We have a value of no and that's associated with churning and that value ended up being **80%**:

1. Here is another way we can look at the relationship between a categorical **Predictor** and a categorical **Outcome** variable. The strongest relationship is between the **Premier** variable and the **Outcome** variable:

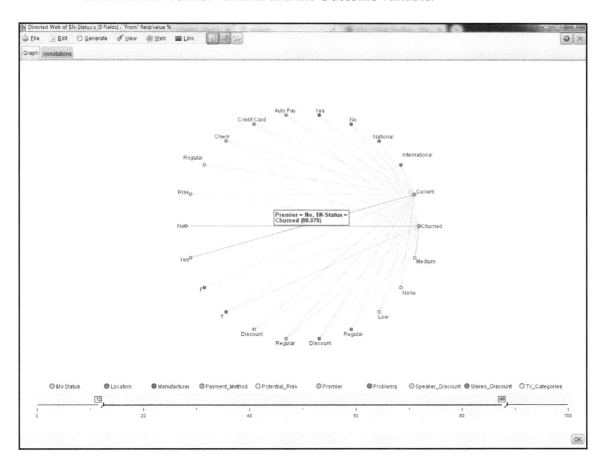

2. Let's look at the relationship between a continuous **Predictor** and a categorical **Outcome** variable. To do that, we are going to go down to the **Graphs** palette and connect the **Select** node to a histogram:

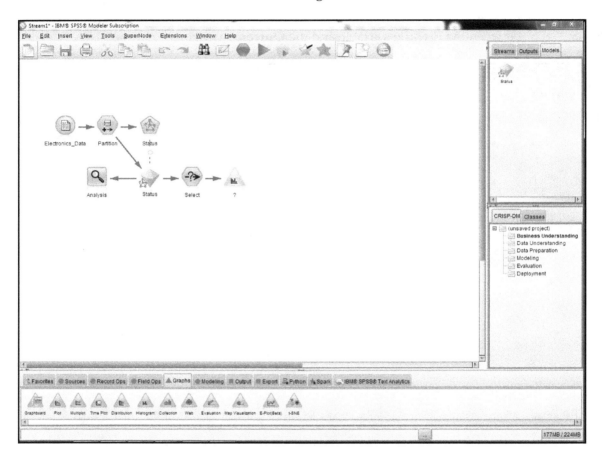

3. Edit the **Histogram,** In the field box, select the **TVs** field . Choose the **TVs** field because this is one of the most important predictors in the mode:

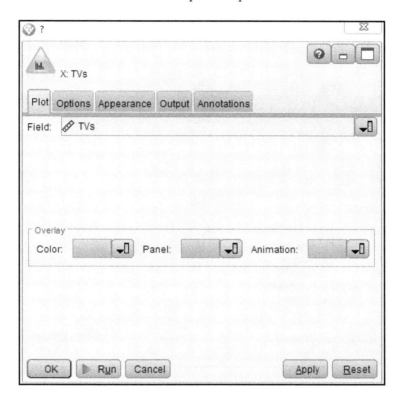

4. In the overlay color box, enter the prediction, which is the variable **$N-Status**:

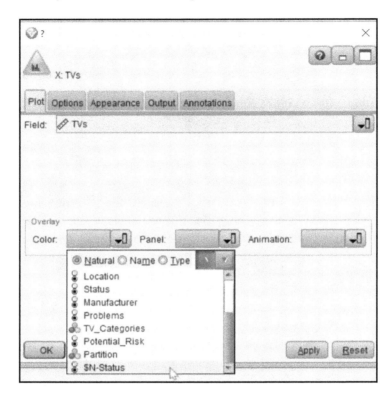

5. Go to the **Options** tab and click on **Normalize by color** to make your comparisons a little easier and click on **Run**:

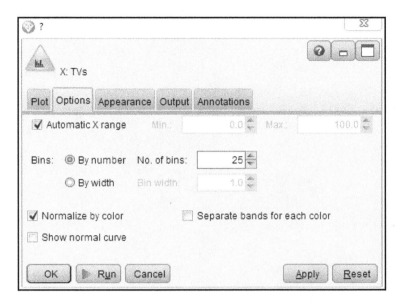

6. We will see the following results:

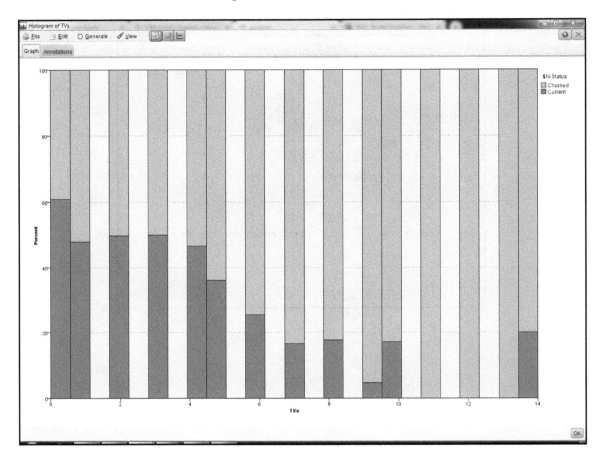

We can see that the blue color is associated with those customers that we predicted we were going to lose. The red color is associated with those customers that we predicted we were going to keep. Notice that the people who bought fewer **TVs** we are predicting about 50%; basically that we're going to end up keeping these customers. As customers are buying more **TVs**, we're predicting that we're going to lose these customers. So that's how this variable is being used by the model, the model is depicting that if you're not buying many **TVs** there's about an equal chance that we're going to keep or lose you as a customer, but if you're buying a lot of **TVs** then we think that we're more likely to lose you as a customer.

In this example, we're going to look at the relationship between two continuous variables:

Let's work with a different dataset. Bring in the **Var. File** node:

1. Edit this node and link it up to a dataset. Navigate to where our dataset, `Bank_Data` is located Select the file:

2. Open the dataset. It's a comma-delimited file, as shown in the following screenshot:

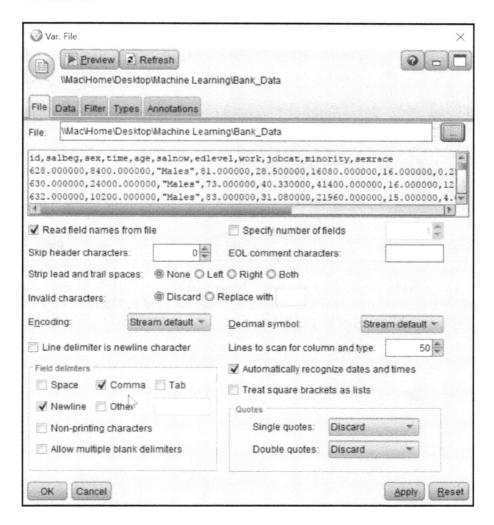

3. Go to the **Types** tab and click on **Read Values** and then select **OK. You will see your variables**:

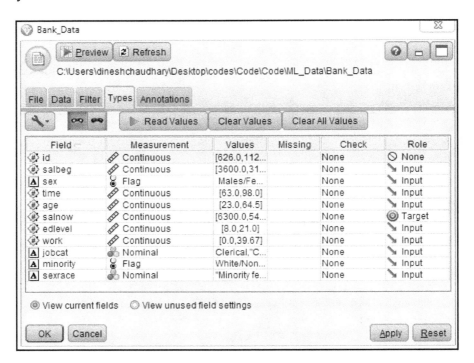

`salnow` is our dependent variable. Hence make sure that it is a target variable. IF it isn't, then change its role to target. Set the role of **id** to **None**. All the other variables are going to be predictors for the current salary variable. Click on **OK**

4. Let's look at the relationship between our outcome variable, which happens to be a continuous variable, and another continuous variable, which is a predictor. Go to the **Graphs** palette and connect the source node to the **Plot** node:

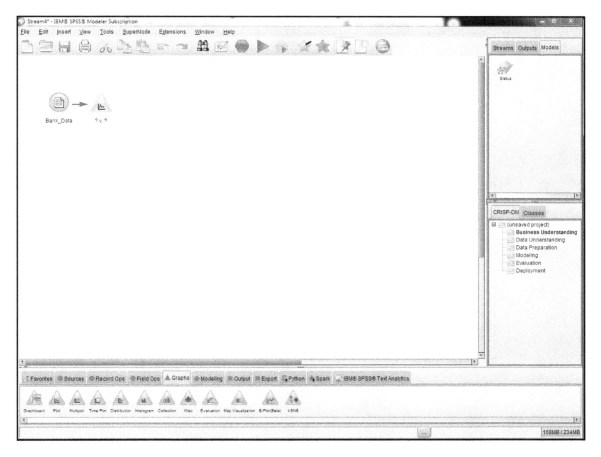

The **Plot** node will allow us create a scatter plot. So, let's edit the **Plot** node.

5. In the **X field** box, we will input our predictor and here we will add the education level, which is the number of years of education that a person has and in the **Y field** box, we will add our outcome variable which is **salnow**, that is, the current salary:

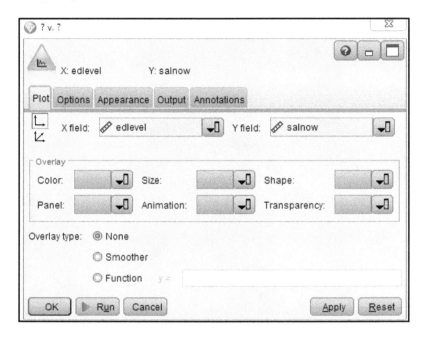

6. Click on **Run** and we get the following graph as the result:

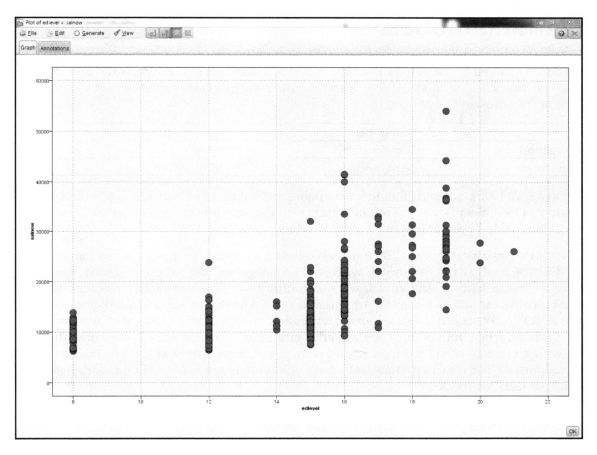

You can see that as the number of years of education increases, the current salary increases too. We have a positive linear relationship, which means that as one variable increases the other variable increases as well, so more education ends up leading to higher current salary, and less education is associated with a lower current salary.

So, this is a way in which we can represent the relationship between two continuous variables. In the next section, we will see how to use statistical tests to interpret the results of a machine learning model.

Using statistics to interpret machine learning models

In this section, we will be using statistics to interpret the results of a machine learning model. We talked about graphs and how they allow us to see and interpret the predictions of a machine learning model, but we can also use those graph for statistical tests. Have a look at the following table:

	Categorical	Continuous
Categorical	Chi-square	ANOVA
Continuous	ANOVA	Correlation

Let's say we had a categorical outcome variable and we had a categorical predictor, we could use the chi-square test. The chi-square test of Independence will allow us to look at the relationship between two categorical variables.

Also, if we have a categorical outcome variable and a continuous predictor, we can use ANOVA to analyze the variance. If we have two categories that we're comparing, we can have a t-test instead, which will allow us to interpret what's going on. On the other hand, if our outcome variable is a continuous variable and we have a categorical predictor, we can use ANOVA. We could also use logistic regression or discriminant analysis if we wanted. And finally, when both of our variables are continuous variables, we can use correlation or linear regression. Let's take a look at a few examples. We will outline some of these techniques so that we can understand what's going on, in terms of the inner workings of a machine learning model.

Let's take a look at how some tables can help clarify relationships between our variables and to see how these different predictors are used by a model.

Go to the **Output** palette and connect the Select node to a matrix node:

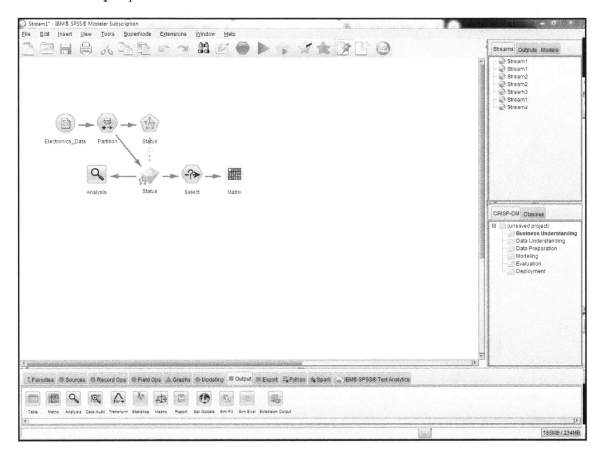

The **Matrix** node will allow us to do the chi-square test, which will help us to look at the relationship between two categorical variables. In this case, we're going to look at the relationship between a categorical predictor and a categorical outcome variable. Let's edit the **Matrix** node. In the **Rows** field, we will input our prediction, which is the **$N-Status** variable and in the **Columns** field, we will select the important predictor in the model, which will be the **Premier** variable:

Go to the **Appearance** tab and select **Percentage of columns**, which means we will get the column percentages and click on Run:

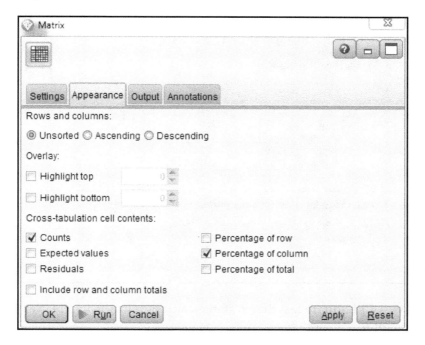

We will get the following result:

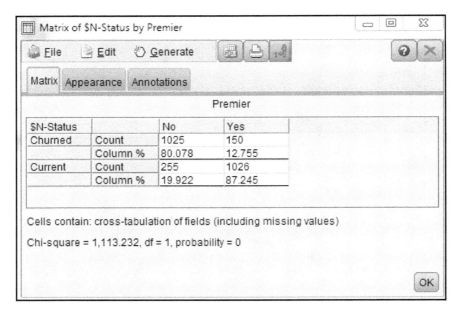

We actually have a **Chi-square** test that is statistically significant, so Premier is an important predictor in the model.

We also get some numerical information that is backing up what we have seen in our graphs previously . We can see that about **80%** of those people, the non-premier customers that are associated with being with **Churned** and about **87%** of the **Premier** customers that are associated with being a **Current** customer.

This is what the model has been doing. Now, we understand how at least one variable is used in the model.

Understanding the relationship between a continuous predictor and a categorical outcome variable

In this section, we are going to look at the relationship between a continuous predictor and a categorical outcome variable. In order to do that, we can either run a t-test or ANOVA and which is also called the **Means** node in Modeler:

1. Connect the **Select** node to the **Means** node from the output palette:

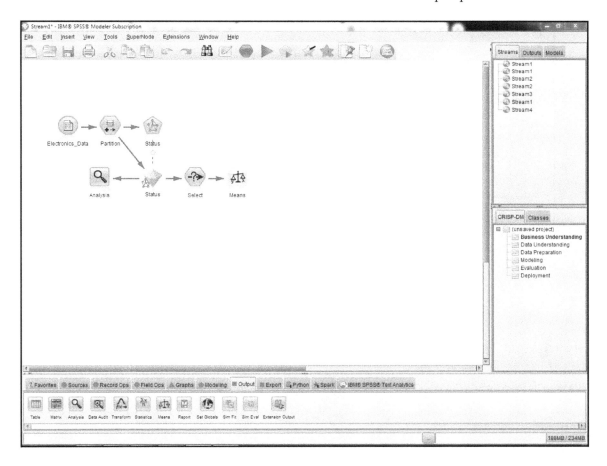

2. Edit the **Means** node. In the **Grouping field** box, input the prediction, which is the **$N-Status** variable:

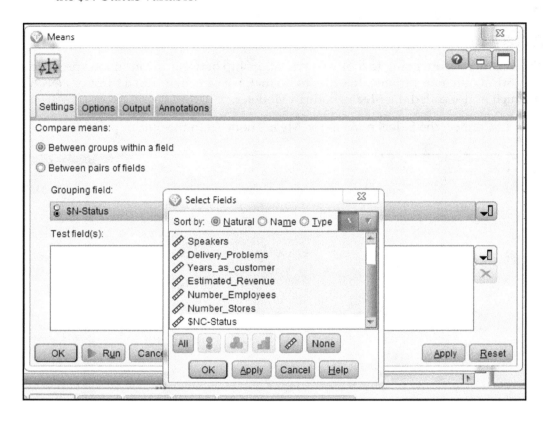

In the **Test field(s)** box, select all of the continuous variables. Also, deselect the actual confidence:

3. Click on **OK** and then click on **Run**. You will get the following output:

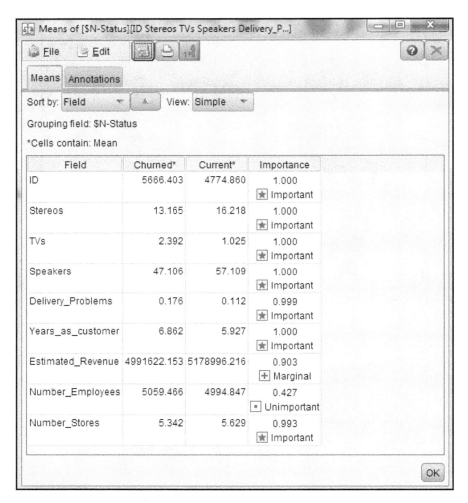

We can see that most of the variables ended up differentiating between the prediction for churn and the prediction for being a current customer. There are some predictors that weren't important. For example, estimated revenue was not statistically significant and neither was the number of employees, but the rest of the predictors were very important.

Now, here we are seeing the **Mean**. But, let's try to find some more information. We'll change the **View** from **Simple** to Advanced and we will get the following results:

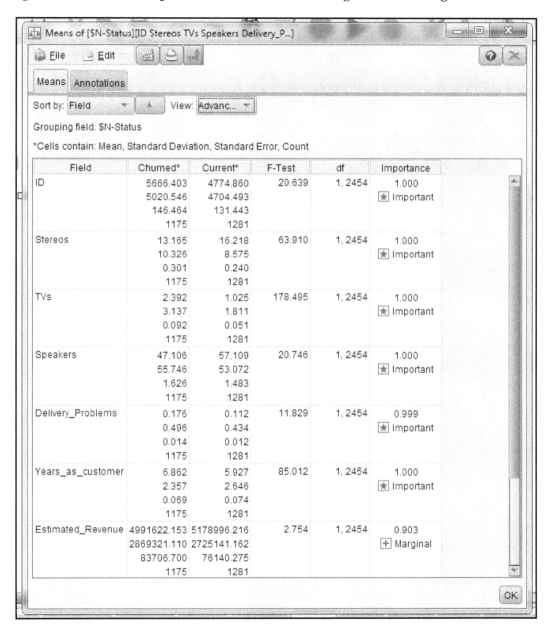

As you can see, we have the same number of cases for each of these variables. The most important predictor ended up being the **TVs** variable, as we can see in the following screenshot, and that's the one that's able to differentiate these groups the most.

For example look at the TVs field, we can see that the current customers are the people who we predicted to churn and we thought we're going to lose these customer, on average they bought 2.4 **TVs**. This prediction is significantly more than the people who were predicted to be going to stay as current customers which bought about one TV on average As we can see, we had a statistically significant result. The opposite is true when it comes to **Stereos**. You can see that we have a statistically significant result, however you can see that the people that we'd predicted to lose as customers on average, bought **13.2** stereos, whereas the people that we'd predicted were going to stay as customers on average bought **16.2** stereos

The last thing we're going to do is look at the relationship between two continuous variables. Earlier, we used the scatter plot to show the relationship between two continuous variables. Here, we're going to quantify that by calculating a correlation:

1. Using the bank dataset, go to the **Output** palette in Modeler and connect the **Statistics** node to source node:

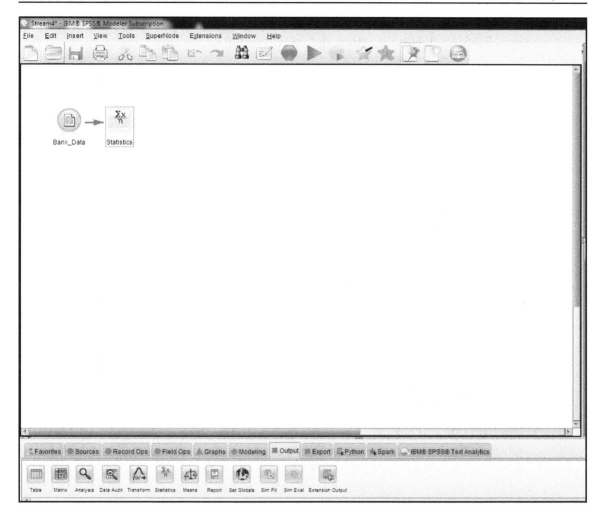

2. Edit the **Statistics** node, which allows us to get summary statistics in the examine box. Click on the fields option and select current salary:

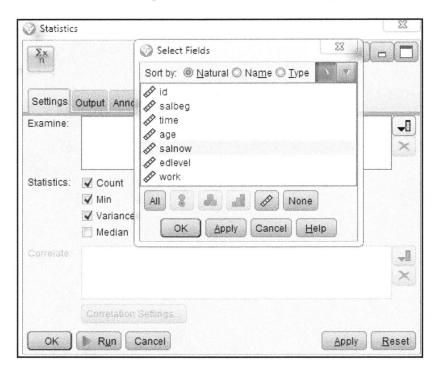

3. Click on **OK** and correlate current salary with the other continuous variables. Click on the arrow next to the correlate box and select the ruler icon, which will select all our continuous variables:

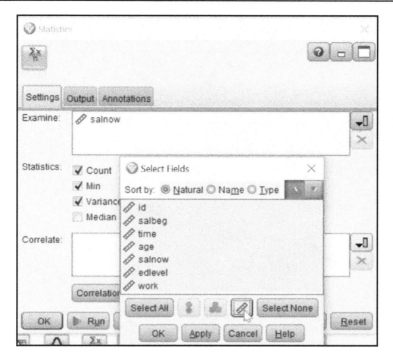

4. Hold down the *Ctrl* key and deselect **id**:

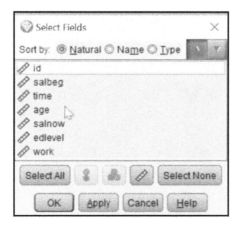

5. Click on **OK** and then click on **Run.** You will see the following result:

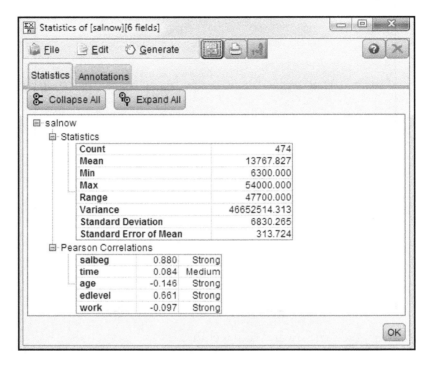

As we can see that the current salary correlates very highly with the starting salary:

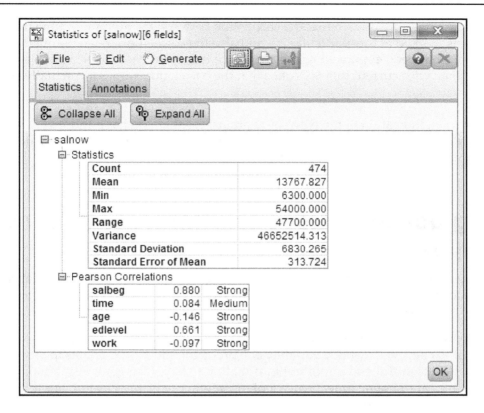

Remember that correlation values can range anywhere from -1 to +1. The farther away the value is from zero, the stronger the relationship. If the correlation coefficients are positive, this means that as the value of one variable increases, the value of the other variable increases. If the correlation coefficients are negative, this means that as the value of one variable increases, the value of the other variable decreases.

Notice that the correlation between beginning salary and current salary is very high, almost 0.9. You can also see that the correlation between education law and current salary is also very high, at 0.66.

On the other hand, you can see that the correlation between the amount of time that someone has worked at this particular job and also the correlation of the number of months that someone has been employed before they have this current job, those variables don't really correlate with current salary. Notice that the correlation values are actually pretty close to zero.

This gives us an indication of the types of relationships that you have and it allows us to quantify those relationships. In the next section, we are going to see how to use decision trees to interpret the results of a machine learning model.

Using decision trees to interpret machine learning models

In this section, we're going to take the predictions from a machine learning model, and use those predictions as our outcome variables. Then we will use the original predictors to understand what's going on, that is, the logic behind the machine learning model.

Previously, we saw that we could use different graphs and tables to figure out how to look at relationships between just one variable, one predictor and how it relates to an outcome variable, which is useful and important information to have. But generally, a model uses many variables at the same time. Hence looking at one predictor is useful, but it doesn't exactly give us a complete picture.

Another technique would be to use a decision tree model to help us understand the logic behind a neural net model, or any kind of machine learning model.

Here, we will be taking our predictions from the model and use that prediction as our outcome variable. Then, we will start with our predictions based on the predictors that the model used:

1. Go to the **Field Ops** palette and connect the generated model to the **Type** node:

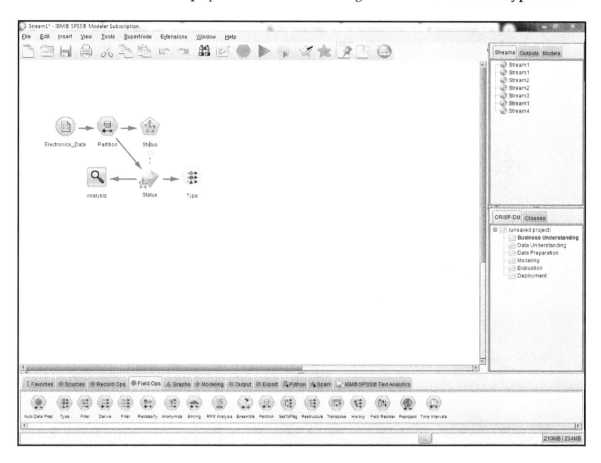

2. Edit the **Type** node and change the role of the original outcome of the **Status** variable. It won't be **Target** anymore since we are going to change its role to **None**. Hence, it won't be included in the model that we are going to build:

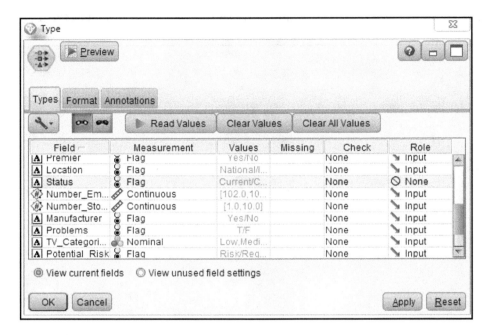

3. Scroll down a little bit. Here, the **$N-Status** prediction is no longer just a prediction or the input; in fact, it will be the **Target** itself. And that's what we are going to predict:

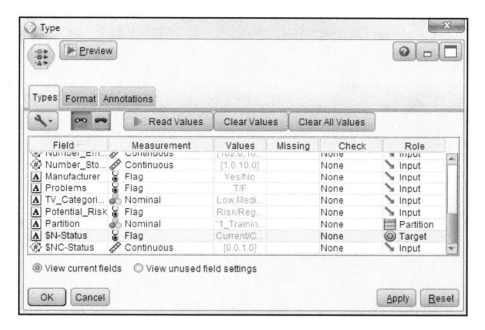

Here, we are trying to get inside the head of a neural net model (or any kind of machine learning model). Take a look at the model's predictions, and use the variables that it used to try to figure out the logic.

4. Remove the confidence value from that prediction since it's not needed. Change its role to **None** and click on **OK**:

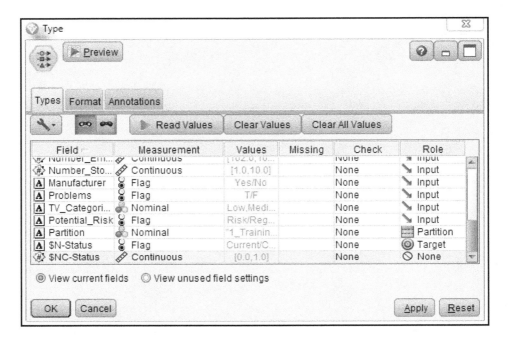

At this point, we have to use another model to understand what happened during the predictions of a machine learning model. We could use a statistical model. But the statistical models have a lot of requirements and assumptions of the data. Also, they can't handle complex interactions and nonlinear relationships very well.

A decision tree model is probably going to do the best job in terms of trying to replicate what the neural net model did:

1. Go to the **Modeling** palette and choose a decision tree model to understand what's going on behind the **Neural Net** model. Connect the **Type** node to **C&R Tree** model:

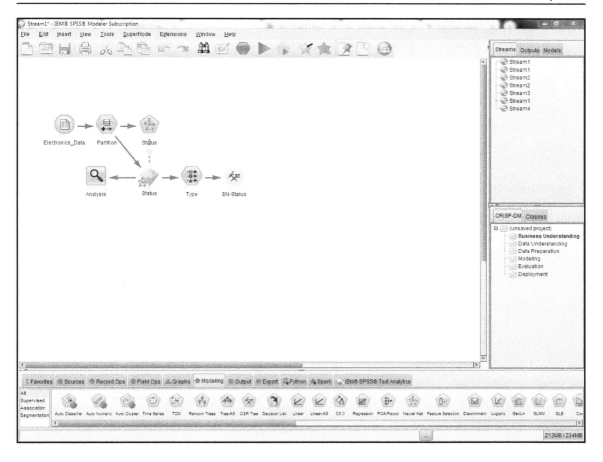

We will be predicting the prediction from the **Neural Net** model.

2. When you edit that model, you will be using all of the predictors that the **Neural Net** model used initially to understand what's going on behind those predictions:

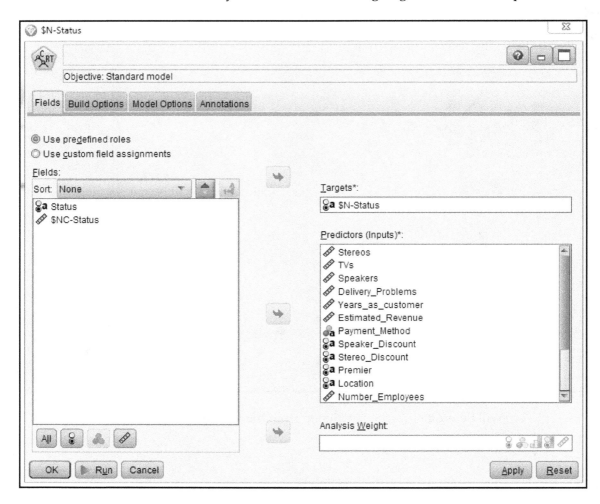

3. Click on **Run**, and have a look at the generated model:

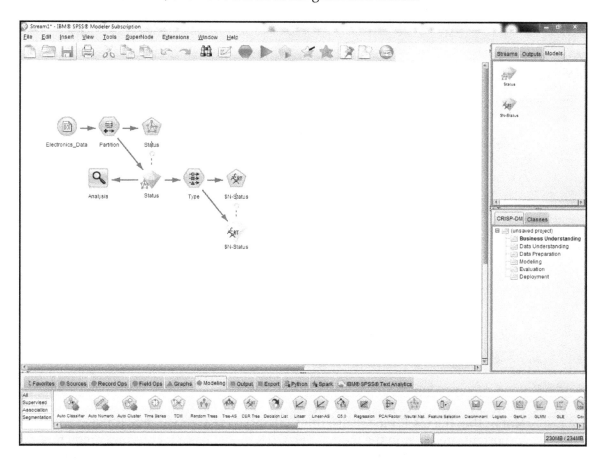

4. We will get the following results:

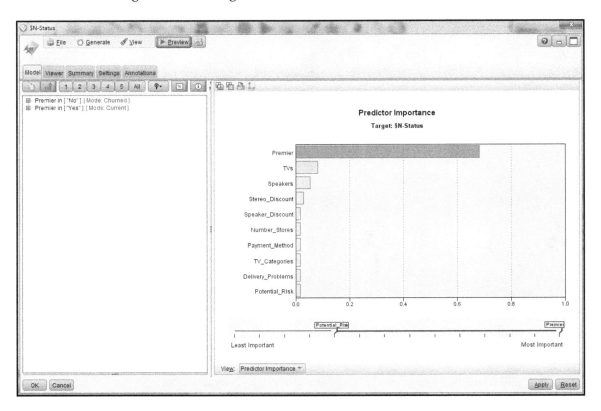

Notice that the **C&R** model also thinks that the **Premier** variable is the most important predictor in the model. The **C&R** model has a lot of same predictors that the neural net model had as the most important predictors. That is important because we want to make sure that we understand the logic of the neural net model (or any machine learning model).

5. Click on the **All** button.

6. Click on the **%** button and we can see some numbers behind these predictions:

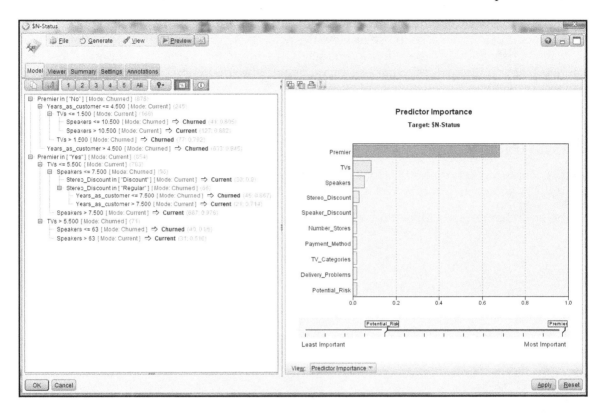

We aren't interested in predicting our outcome variable, **Status** here. Instead, we're trying to understand the reasoning behind the predictions of the neural net model.

Here, you can see that we're using multiple variables. Have a look at the preceding screenshot. The first rule says that if the variable is **Premier**, you had a value of **NO** and you have been a customer of ours for less than or equal to four and a half years, and you bought less than or equal to one and a half TVs, and you bought less than or equal to ten point five speakers, we're predicting that we're going to lose you as a customer. That rule applied to 41 people and the confidence in that rule is about 81%. On the other hand, if all of that same criteria is applied, so that you're still a non-premier customer, you haven't been with us that long as a customer, you've bought very few TVs but you bought more than 10.5 speakers, we're predicting that you're going to be a current customer. That rule applied to 127 people, and the confidence in that rule is 88%.

Now we try to understand the logic as to what potentially the neural net model was doing. It's not exactly the same as what the neural net model did, because the algorithms for a neural net model and a decision tree model are very different. We were just trying to understand the logic behind a neural net model. In this case, we had a whole set of criteria, and it ended up allowing us to use or view the relationship between multiple variables simultaneously and how they end up impacting the prediction. This is just another tool you can use to try to understand what's going on behind the predictions of a machine learning model.

Summary

In this chapter, we started off by looking at different types of prediction models. Then we used these models to interpret the machine learning models.

In the next chapter, we will explore different ways that we can improve individual models.

Improving Individual Models 4

In this chapter, we will see how we can improve different models, and we will see how to modify model options. We will also learn how to use different models and see how we can remove noise by removing predictors that are not really needed for predictions. You will also understand how to prepare additional data for the models, and we will see how we can add additional fields. Finally, you see how how oversampling and undersampling different categories of an outcome variable can make it more likely that the model that you end up using actually better understands the data.

The following are the topics that will be covered in this chapter, and these are the ways in which models can be improved:

- Modifying model options
- Using different models
- Removing noise
- Doing additional data preparation
- Balancing data (oversampling/undersampling)

Modifying model options

Modifying model options to improve the model is one of the straightforward ways to improve a model. We will see how we can do this with the help of an example:

> 1. We will create an **SVM** model just as we did in the second chapter:

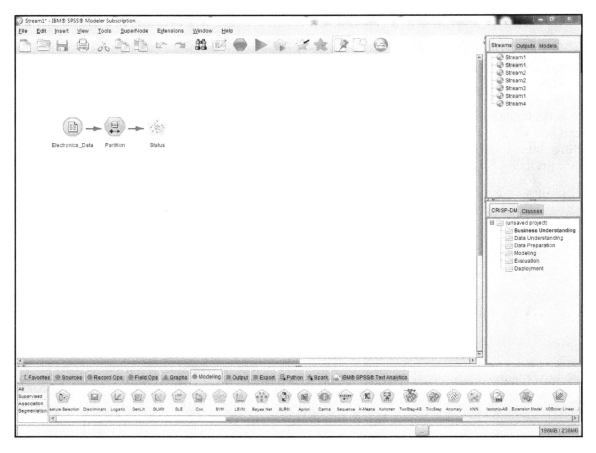

> 2. Click on **Status**, go to the **Expert** tab, and select **Expert** under **Mode**. As we have seen in Chapter 2, *Getting Started with Machine Learning*, whenever we are using **SVM** models, we need to modify their settings. Change the **Regularization parameter** to **5**. And, in the **Kernel type**, select **Polynomial**. Then, click on **Run**.

3. You will see a model created. Now, let's do our next step of analyzing the model. Connect your generated model to an **Analysis** node from the **Output** palette. Open the **Analysis** node, and select the **Coincidence matrices** (for the symbolic targets option) and click on **Run**. This will be the result that will be acquired:

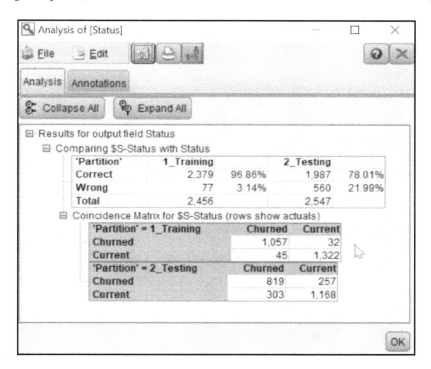

The results clearly show that the model isn't consistent as there is a huge difference between the accuracy percentage of the training and the testing dataset. But, what we can see is the testing percentage is better than the testing percentage that we acquired for the linear model in Chapter 2, *Getting Started with Machine Learning*, around 73%. Hence, maybe the polynomial model can do a better job but not with the current model as it is capitalizing on chance.

Now that we have a potentially better model, we can go ahead and modify the settings of this model. You can go to the **SVM** model status, and in the **Expert** tab, you can see that the **Degree** is set to **3**. There is a chance that this cubic function may be proving a bit complex for the data that we have. Let's use a quadratic function instead. Change the **Degree** to **2** and click **Run**.

Again, run the analysis just like we have always done, and you will find these results:

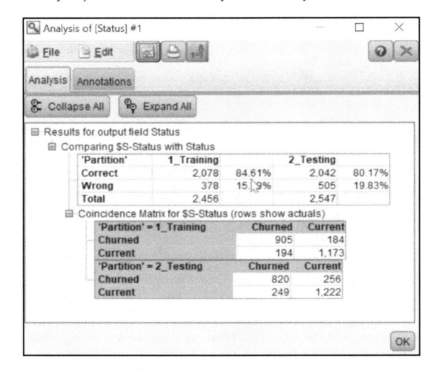

As you can see, the accuracy percentages of both the datasets are within a difference of 5%. Hence, we can say that the model is consistent. Moreover, we can also see that the overall accuracy for the testing dataset has improved.

This is how we improved an existing model by modifying its options to provide better results with higher overall accuracy and consistency.

Using a different model to improve results

In the previous section, we saw how we can improve a result acquired from the model by modifying its options. Now, we will see how to improve the results by changing the model itself.

Every model looks at the data differently. They have their own algorithms. These algorithms provide us with different perspectives to look at the data. Sometimes, just changing the perception of looking at the data can give us improved results. The different algorithms capitalize on unique aspects of data. Let's see how we can do this with the help of an example:

1. Bring your data, and partition it into training and testing datasets.
2. Connect the **Partition** node to a **Neural Net** node from the **Modeling** palette:

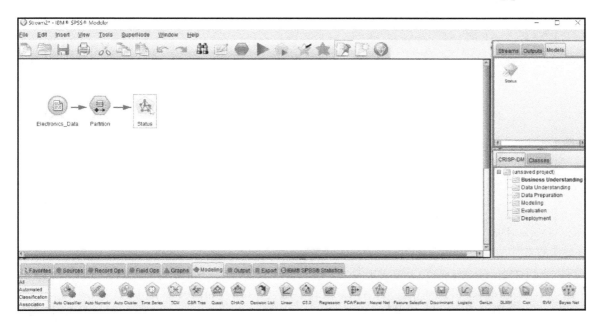

3. Click on the **Neural Net** node and go to the **Build Options** tab. In this, go the **Advanced** option and just change the **Random seed** to 5000:

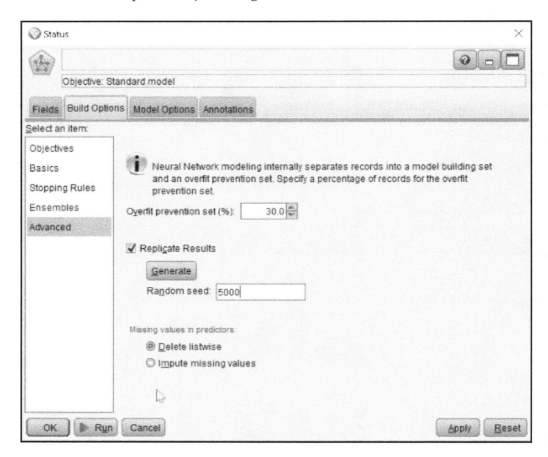

4. The reason that we are keeping the seed as 5000 is because we have acquired a better result using 5000 as the seed, as you may can recall from Chapter 2, *Getting Started with Machine Learning,* where we have demonstrated a neural network.

5. Click on **Run**.

6. Once again, you will have to analyze the model that is built. For this, recall the steps that we have followed until now. Go to the **Output** palette, and connect the generated model node to the **Analysis** node. Run the **Analysis** node with the checked **Coincidence matrices**. The following will be the results acquired:

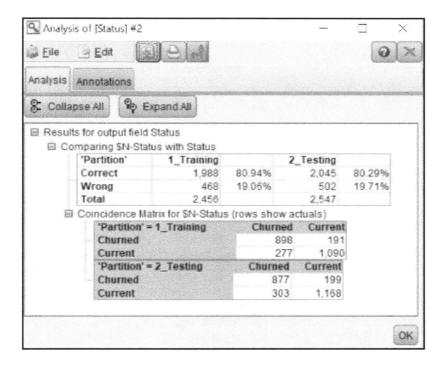

7. You can see that we are at an overall accuracy of around 80%, and how each of the predictions have performed. The overall accuracy is similar to what we have achieved when we used the **SVM** model. Hence, we can say that the **SVM** and **Neural Net** models are doing equally well for this dataset. Let's see how we can improve these results a little more.

8. We will use a decision tree in this example. For adding a decision tree node, select the **Partition** node, and connect it to the **C5.0** node from the **Modeling** palette:

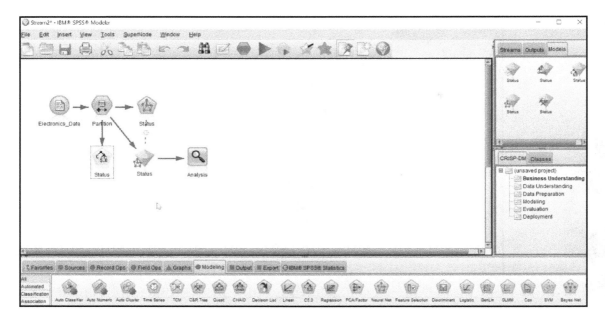

The **C5.0** model is a decision tree model that looks at the data from a very different perspective.

9. Click on the **C5.0** model node to build a **C5.0** model and run it:

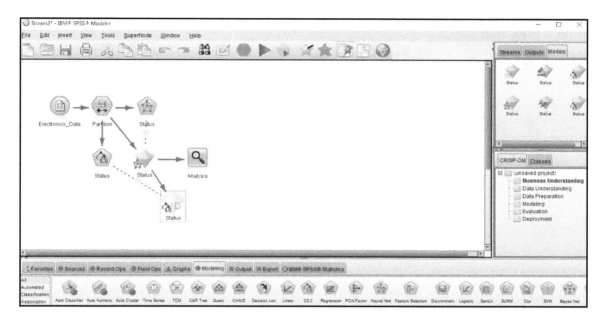

10. Now, connect the **C5.0** model node to the **Neural Net** generated model node.

11. Connect the **C5.0** generated model to the **Analysis** node:

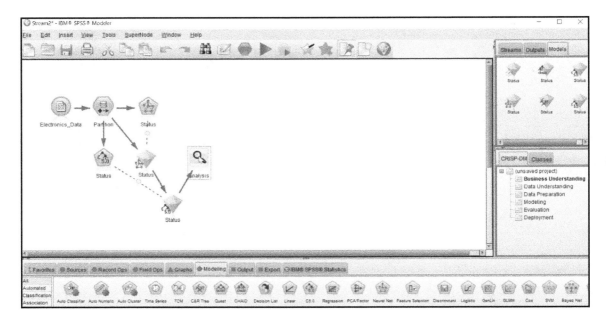

This will enable us to compare the results very easily.

12. Run the **Analysis** node. The following will be the results acquired:

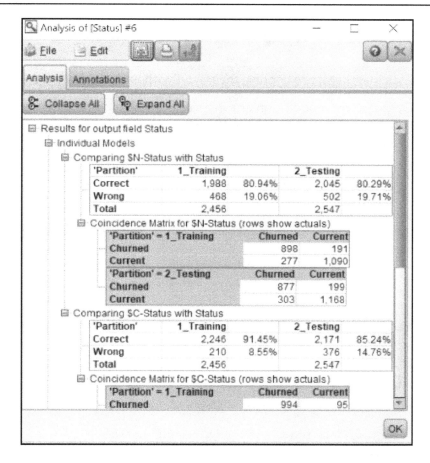

As you can see, the overall accuracy for the testing dataset with the **C5.0** model is 85%. This is much better than what we had acquired with just the **Neural Net** model. We can certainly improve on this by making some modifications to the **C5.0** model, which I'll leave up to you as a homework exercise.

So, we saw how the **C5.0** model slightly improved the results, and has done a good job in overall accuracy and with each of the predictions both for the training and testing dataset. This was just an example on another approach to improve the performance of a model. We will now see how removing noise from the data can give us much better results.

Removing noise to improve models

Let's focus on how noise can affect the results. Noise is nothing but missing data, outliers, or too many predictors that try to confuse the model with unnecessary predictions.

 Decision tree models don't have noise because of too many predictors, as by default, they eliminate the predictors that they don't use for predictions as opposed to other statistical and machine learning models.

Having too many predictors in a model causes the following problems:

- Additional noise in the data that affects the overall accuracy of the model
- The model becomes much more complex than it should be
- If new data is to be added for new predictions, we need to collect data even for the variables that are not important and are not really required for the predictions, because our model uses them up to a certain extent.

If these kinds of predictors are cleared and eliminated from the model, this could simplify the understanding of the model and, potentially, it will give better results as well.

How to remove noise

Let's understand with the help of an example. Follow these steps:

1. Partition your data into a training and testing dataset.
2. Connect your **Partition** node to a **Neural Net** model from the **Modeling** palette.
3. Select the model and, just like we have always done, go to the **Build Options** tab, then to the **Advanced** options, and change the **Random seed** to `5000` (because that has given us the best results so far). Click on **Run**.
4. We have seen the accuracy of this model before. Refer to the list of top 10 predictors for different random seeds that we acquired and stored in a table while demonstrating **Neural Net** in `Chapter 2`, *Getting Started with Machine Learning*:

229176228	641835376	1	2552	5000
Speakers	Premier	Premier	Premier	Premier
Premier	Speakers	Years as customer	Stereos	Years as customer
TVs	Years as customer	Speakers	Speakers	Stereos
Stereos	Stereos	TV categories	TVs	TVs
Years as customer	TVs	Stereos	Years as customer	Speakers
Delivery problems	Delivery problems	TVs	Delivery problems	TV categories
TV categories	Estimated revenue	Estimated revenue	Potential Risk	Number employees
Potential risk	TV categories	Payment method	TV categories	Estimated revenue
Estimated revenue	Problems	Number employees	Estimated revenue	Delivery problems
Number employees	Number stores	Delivery problems	Number employees	Problems

We will now remove the variables, which haven't appeared in any of the models or have appeared in just a few.

5. For removing variables, we will create another version of this **Neural Net** model. Connect the **Partition** node to another **Neural Net** model from the **Modeling** palette:

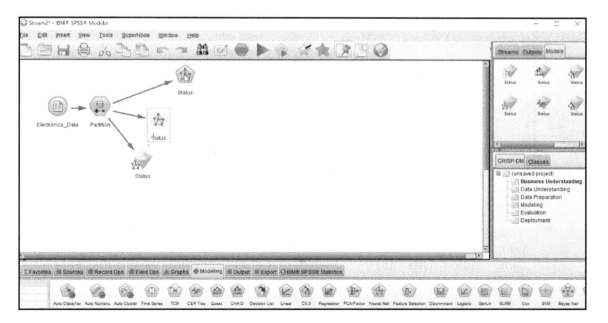

6. Edit the new **Neural Net** model: Here, in the **Fields** tab, we will remove the **Predictors** that didn't appear in the top 10 list of any model:

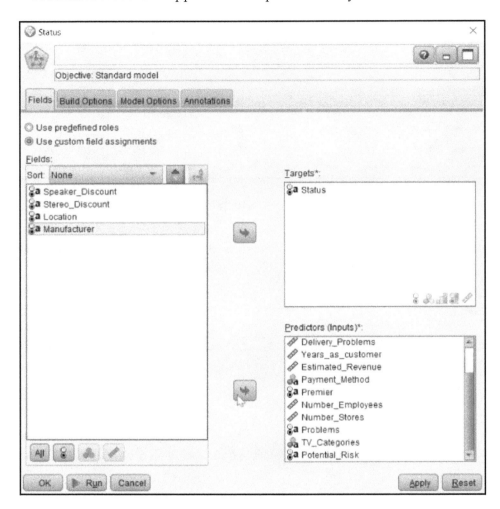

You just have to click the predictor from the **Inputs** list and click on the arrow pointing towards the left-side box. You can also restore them if needed using the same method. These are the variables that didn't appear in the top 10 list of any model.

7. We will also remove the variables that appeared just once or twice in the lists:

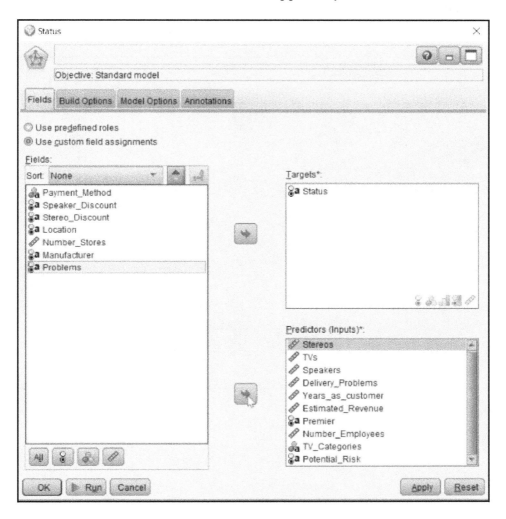

8. Go to the **Advanced** options in the **Build Options** tab and change the **Random seed** to 5000. Then click on **Run**.

9. Connect the first **Neural Net** model to the second **Neural Net** model:

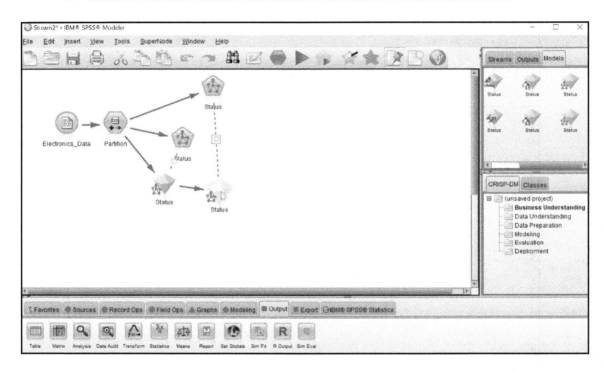

10. Connect the second **Neural Net** model to the **Analysis** node from the **Output** palette:

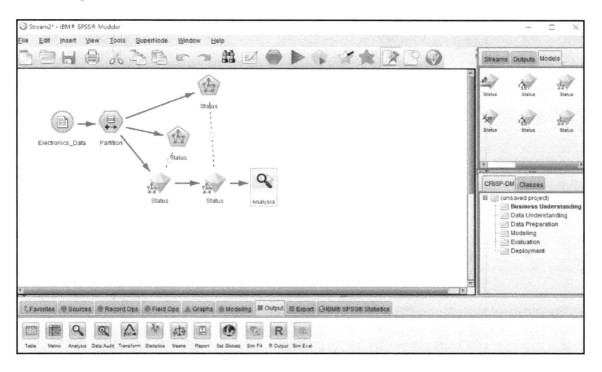

11. Run the **Analysis** node, just like we have always done. The following will be the comparative analysis of the two models:

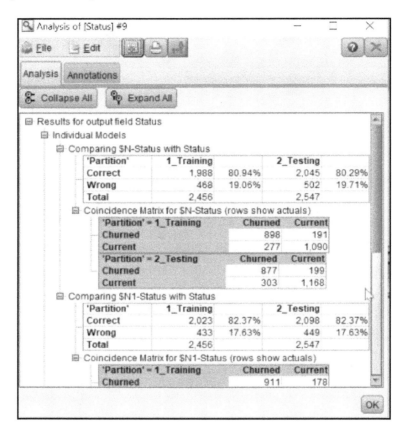

As you can see, the overall accuracy for the testing and training dataset of the second model is slightly better than the first model. Hence, we got a 2% improvement in predictability just by removing some unnecessary predictors. If we see the job of the model in predicting for each of the individual categories, the model with noise removed has done well in that too.

Hence, we have explored another way to improve the results acquired from a model. We saw how removing noise, and reducing the number of variables or predictors by eliminating the unnecessary ones, can give us better results. Let's move on to see another method to improve accuracy. We will see how preparing the data to some extent can give us better results.

Doing additional data preparation

In this section, we will see how additional preparation done on the data can allow us to extract an extra piece of information.

Until now, we have improved our model by modifying its options, using a different model, changing the perspective of looking at data, and removing noise. Sometimes though, these techniques will just slightly improve the model; but if you could go back to the data preparation phase and look for extra bits that can be pulled from the data that can give better results, this can really go a long way in improving accuracy.

Preparing the data

Follow these steps to prepare the data in the data preparation stage:

1. Get your data and partition it.
2. Run a **Neural Net** model again, with a **Random seed** of 5000. We will get an accuracy of around 80%.
3. We will now create a new model and add one additional predictor. If you go back to the list of top ten predictors list, we will find predictors such as the number of speakers and TVs that customers purchased. Hence, it makes sense to have a predictor that shows the total number of items purchased.

4. Go to the **Field Ops** palette and connect the **Partition** node to a **Derive** node:

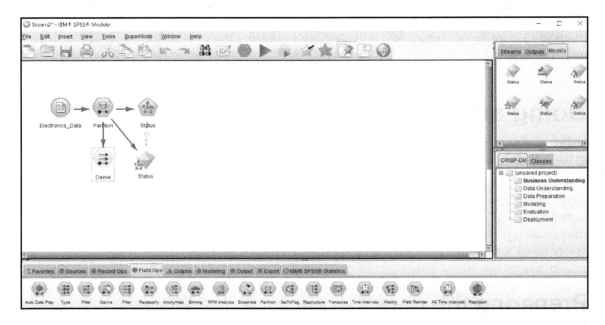

A **Derive** node allows us to create additional variables.

5. Edit the **Derive** node. Set the **Derive field** as `Total Items` and click on the expression builder button, which is on the right of the **Formula** field, and we will create an expression by selecting the predictors of interest and clicking on the plus button:

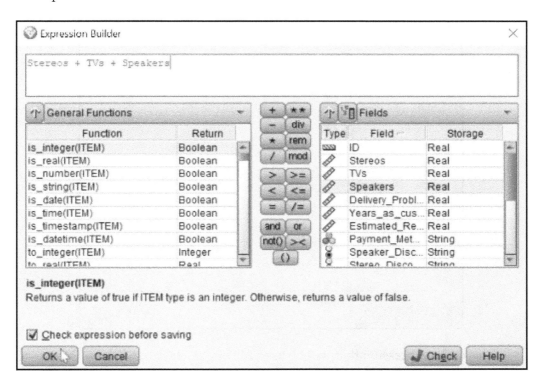

This means that `Total Items` includes **Stereos**, **TVs**, and **Speakers**. You will get an expression in the **Formula** field, like this:

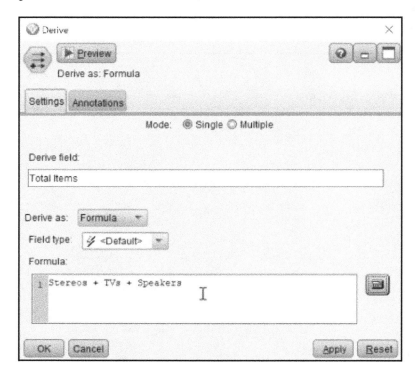

This is the expression that will be used for `Total Items`. Click on **OK**.

6. The variable that we just created needs to be instantiated so that the model is able to use it; for this, connect the **Total Items** node to the **Type** node from the **Field Ops** palette:

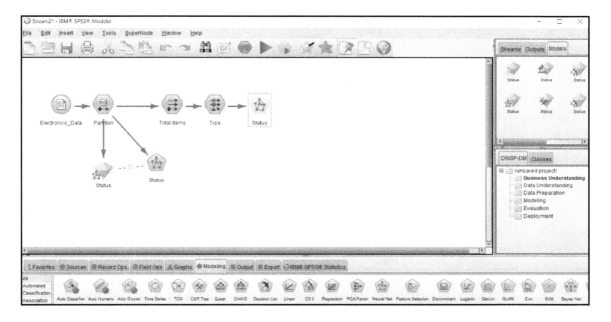

7. Edit the **Type** node. Click on the **Read Values** button to read the new variable:

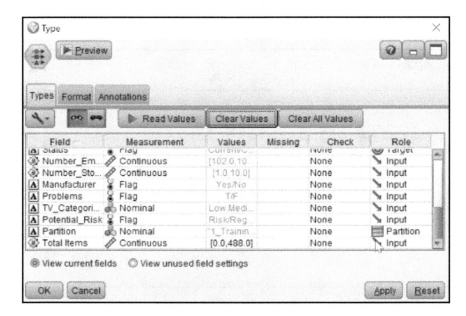

As you can see, the **Total Items** predictor is now read, and that it will be counted as an **Input** predictor in this model. Click on **OK.**

8. Connect the **Type** node to a **Neural Net** model from the **Modeling** palette:

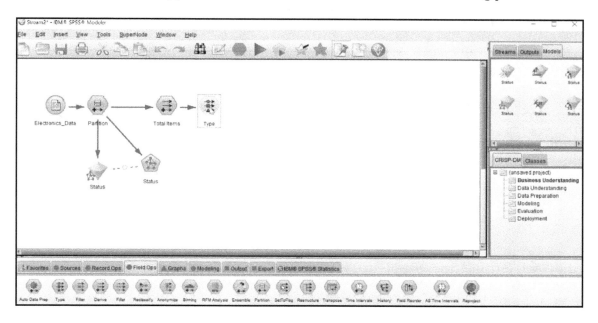

9. Run the **Neural Net** model with **Random seed** set to 5000.

10. Take a look at the model results by clicking on the newly generated model. You can see that the **Total Items** has acquired its place in the top ten predictors in **Predictor Importance**:

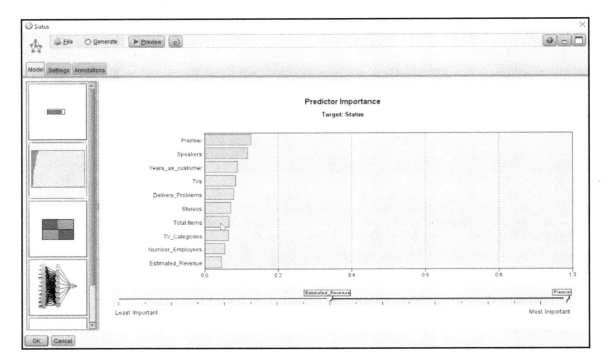

Close the window.

11. We will now connect the first generated model to the second model:

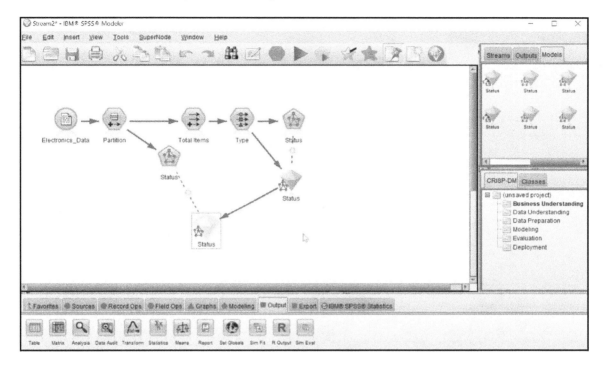

12. Add an **Analysis** node to the first **Neural Net** model:

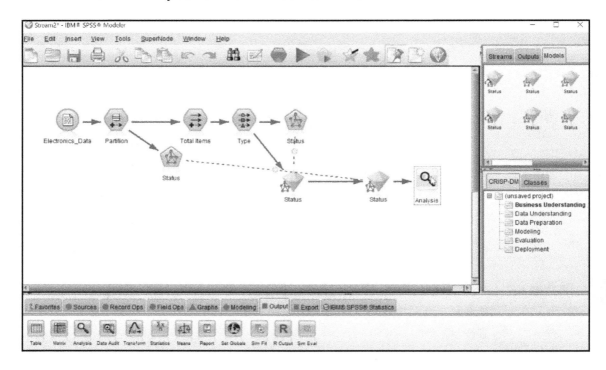

13. Run the **Analysis** node, as always. You should get the following results:

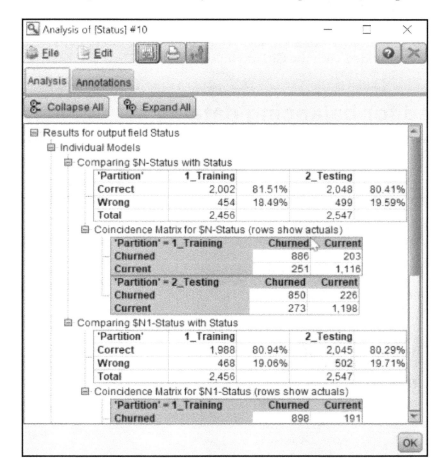

Notice that the accuracy that we have has slightly improved. We just added a variable to an existing model. Hence, we get an idea of how our results can be affected when we do additional preparation on the data before running the model.

Speaking of how **Total Items** has helped the model, you can see the job it has done for predicting current customers. We have actually done a better job in predicting the current customer field. Hence, this shows that the new variables that we chose to add may not necessarily improve the accuracy of the overall model, but can certainly improve the accuracy of one or more predicted categories. You can decide which category is more important for your requirements and select a new variable accordingly. We will now move on to see how sampling can help us provide better results.

Balancing data

In this section, we will see how we can oversample or undersample different aspects of the outcome variable to improve our accuracy. We will change our dataset to see this. Refer to the `Loan` dataset provided with the GitHub link of this book.

The need for balancing data

To demonstrate this, we will use a different dataset. Select the **Var. File** node on the canvas. Navigate to where the file is located by clicking the triple dots beside the file field. Then select the `Loan` dataset:

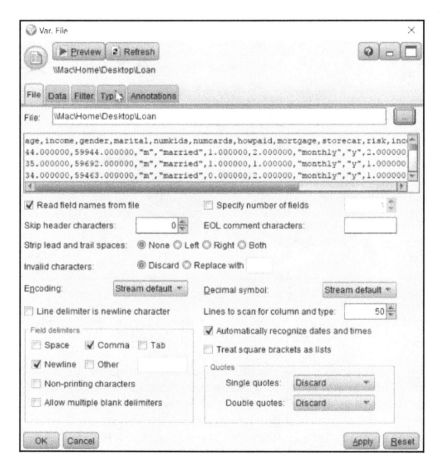

Go to the **Types** tab and change the **Loan** predictor's **Role** to **Target**. This is the variable that we will predict:

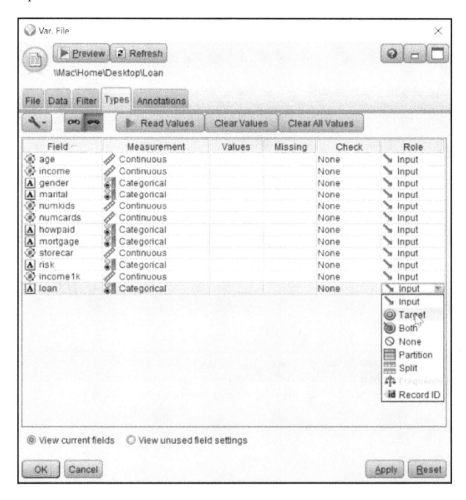

Click on **Read Values**. Then, click on **OK**. In this example, we are predicting whether or not people have a loan.

Let's see the distribution of our loan variable; go to the **Graphs** palette and connect our source node, **Loan**, to a **Distribution** node:

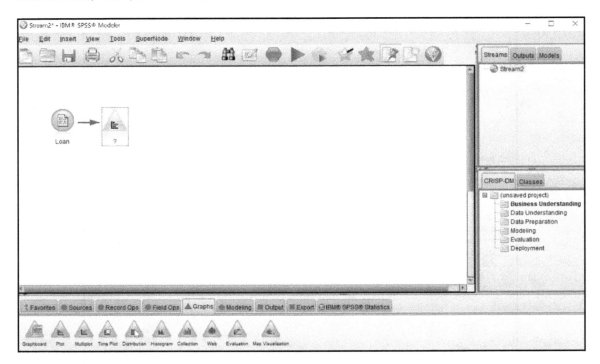

Click on the **Distribution** node. Then click on the arrow next to the field box to select our predictor, for which we need to see the distribution, in our case, **loan**:

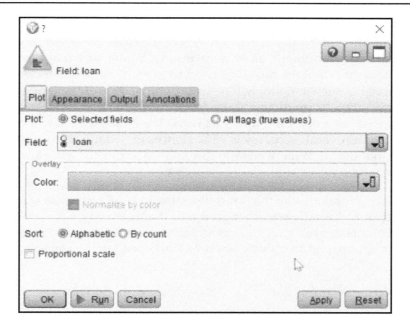

Then, click on **Run**. You will see the following distribution:

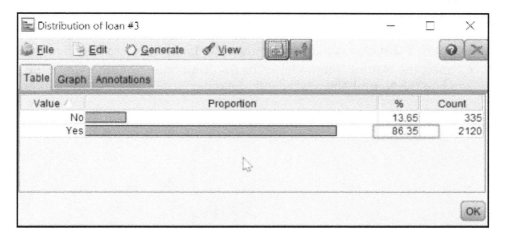

Notice that 86% of the people in this dataset have a loan, and 13% don't have a loan. In such a case, predicting the group of people having no loan can be a little difficult because the distribution is very uneven. Hence, in such a situation, we need to balance the data. This means making it a little more similar similar in terms of the category size of each group. This balancing of data is also known as oversampling or undersampling.

Let's take a little more of an extreme example. Let's say that we're trying to predict fraud, and that the distribution of the dataset is that 99% of the cases are perfectly legitimate and only 1% of the cases are fraudulent. Now, if we build a model with that type of distribution, what will often happen is that the model is going to predict that all cases aren't fraudulent. The overall accuracy of such a model will be 99%, because 99% of the time it's right, but what we really care about is predicting those few fraudulent cases. If we're always predicting that we have a good case, then you know the model itself is not really that useful, even though its overall accuracy is 99%. Hence, sometimes the overall accuracy of the model is not that useful. What we really care more about is the accuracy of predicting each individual category.

What happens with situations like the fraud detection example is, because one group is so over-represented, or technically the other group, or the smaller group, is under-represented, the model doesn't really learn the patterns or the characteristics that are going on for the smaller group, and that's why we sometimes need to oversample or undersample.

Let's come back to our example and try and see what we can do with it.

Implementing balance in data

Let's first build a model to predict the loan and see what we find:

1. Go to the **Field Ops** palette and connect the **Loan** node to a **Partition** node.
2. Connect the **Neural Net** model to the **Partition** node from the **Modeling** palette, and run the **Neural Net** model with defaults:

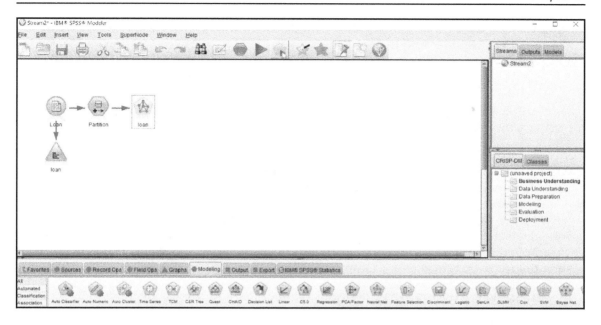

3. Go to the **Output** palette and connect the newly generated node to the **Analysis** node. Run the **Analysis** node with the **Coincidence matrices** checked, and you will get the following results:

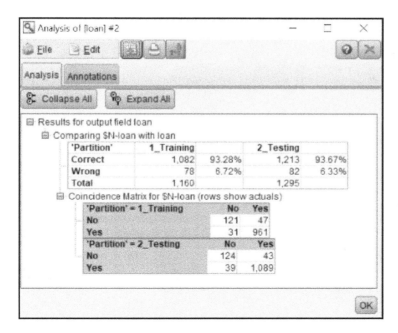

As you can see, the overall accuracy of the model is around 93%, and the model is quite consistent. Let's see how well the model has predicted each one of the categories. We are certainly predicting the **Yes** group pretty well. However, we are not doing so well with the **No** group. We can try to improve the way we predict our **No** group.

The results acquired bring us to a stage where we will have to oversample the **No** group. Or undersample the **Yes** group.

For oversampling, we will first need to partition the dataset into a training and testing dataset. One thing to remember here is when we are oversampling a dataset, we do not need to have equal oversampling on the training as well as the testing dataset. In fact, what we need is to assess the testing dataset on the original distribution, because with oversampling we run the risk of performing well on the training dataset but not on the testing dataset. To avoid this, we will first have to separate our data. Hence, we will first oversample the training dataset data, then build a model on it, and then apply it to the testing dataset:

1. Go to the **Record Ops** palette, and connect the **Partition** node to the **Select** node:

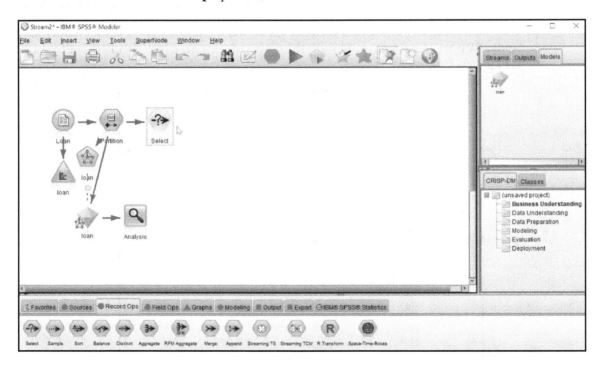

2. Select the **Select** node. Here we will select only the people that are in the training dataset. We will perform our data manipulations, then oversample or undersample our data and get the results. For doing this, click on the expression builder. Then, select the **Partition** variable:

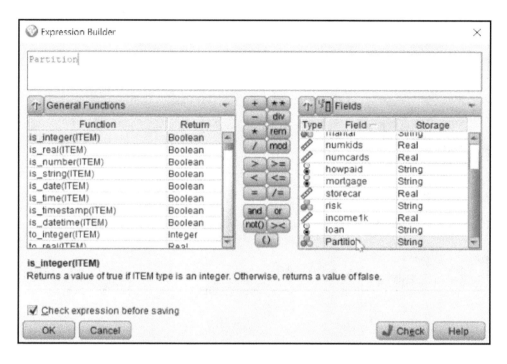

Click on the = sign, and then click on the **field values** button:

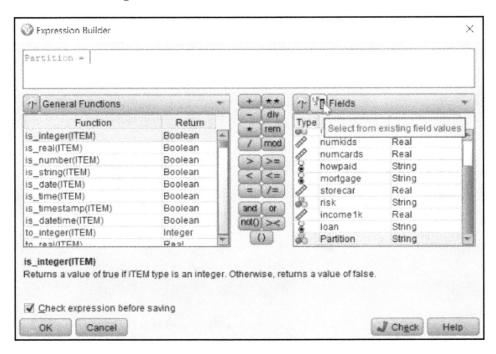

Then, select the **Training** dataset and click on **OK**:

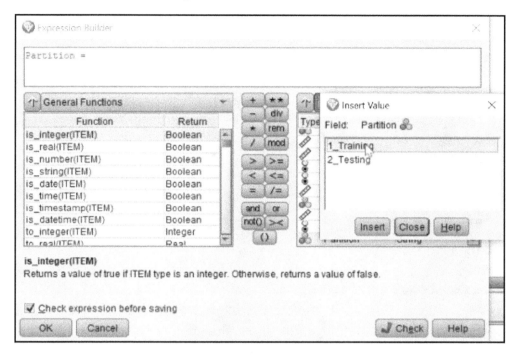

A dialogue box will open. Click **OK** on that too.

3. Connect another **Select** node to the existing **Select** node:

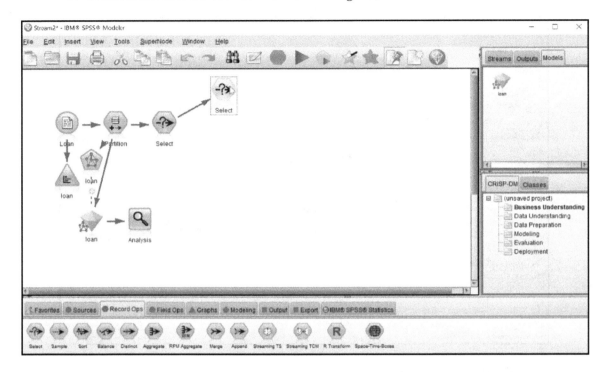

In this **Select** node, we will keep people with a value of **No**; for this, go to the expression builder and select the **loan** variable, click on the = sign, and then click on the field values button and select **No**:

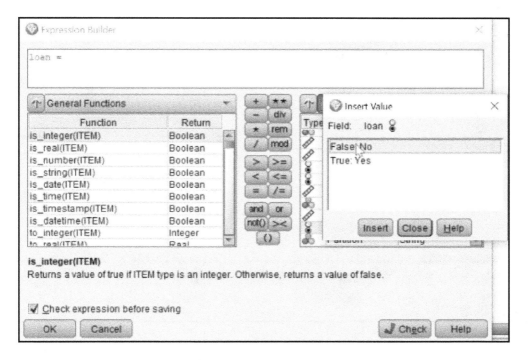

4. We will add another **Select** node connected to the first **Select** node:

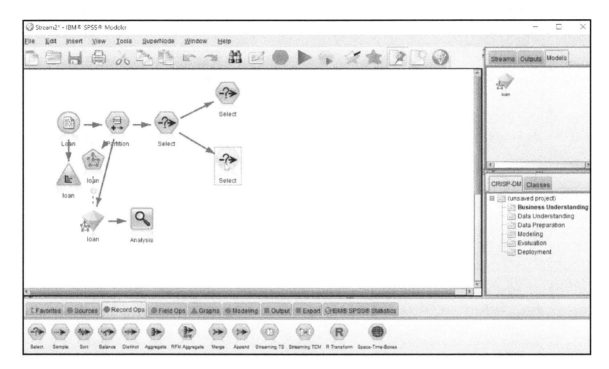

Click on the expression builder. Select the **loan** variable, and click on the = sign. Click on the field values button and select the **Yes** value. Click on **OK**. So, now we have selected all people with a loan. This is a larger group of people, which is over-represented. This brings us to the stage where we select only one-third of the dataset.

5. Go to the **Record Ops** palette and connect the **Sample** node to the **Select** node of the **Yes** group:

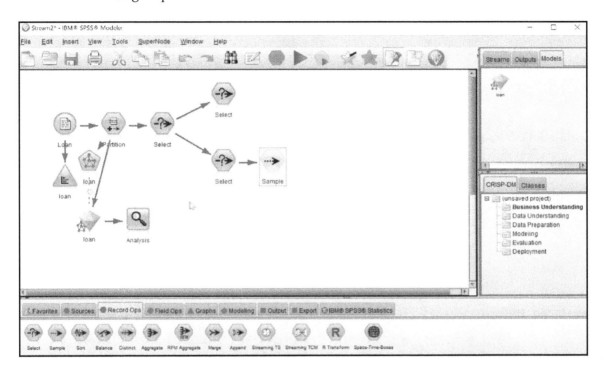

6. Edit the **Sample** node. Select **Random%** to randomly select the values, and set the value to **33%**. Also, check the **Repeatable partition assignment**. This will allow us to select the same people every time we create a model for this selection. Click on **OK**:

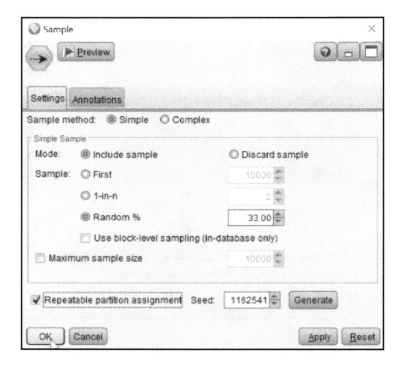

7. We will have to combine this separate data and bring it back together. For this, connect the **Select** node that has all people with the value set as **No** to the **Append** node. Then right-click on the **Sample** node and select connect to connect it to the **Append** node:

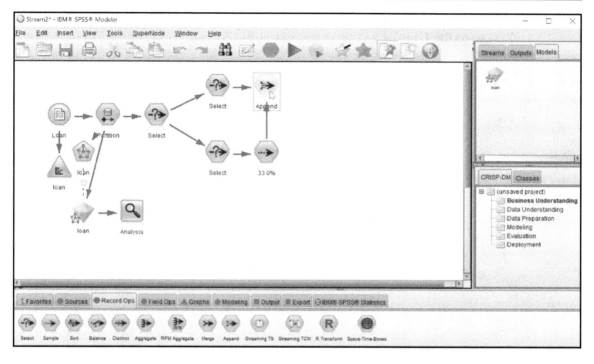

8. Click on the **Append** node and select **All datasets**, then click on **OK**:

9. Let's check how the distribution of the **Loan** field looks now after sampling. For this, go to the **Graphs** palette and connect the **Append** node to the **Distribution** node:

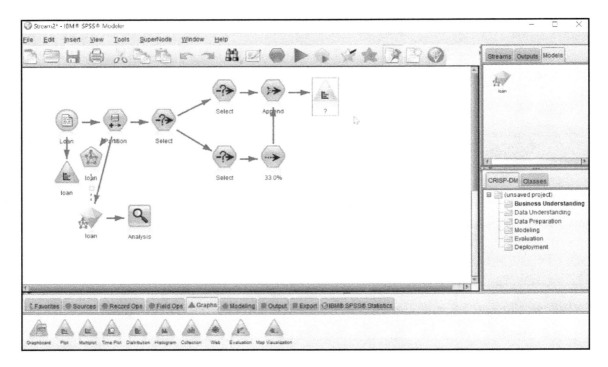

10. Click on the **Distribution** node, go to the **Field** box, and select **loan** just as we did before. Then click on **Run**. Here is the distribution that we have acquired after sampling:

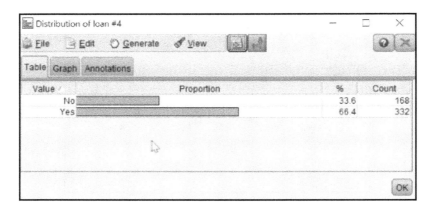

You can see that the **No** group constitutes about one-third of the sample.

Hence, by undersampling the **Yes** node, we were able to see the difference from 13%.

Let's see oversampling:

1. Let's now connect the Append node to the Type node from the Field Ops palette. Here, we won't be using the partition field. Hence, go to the Types node and change the Partition's role to None.

2. We will again build our model by going to the modeling palette. And connect the Type node to a neural net model. And run this setup on the defaults.

3. Now, connect your first generated model to the newly generated model, and connect both of them to the Analysis node. Let's see our results:

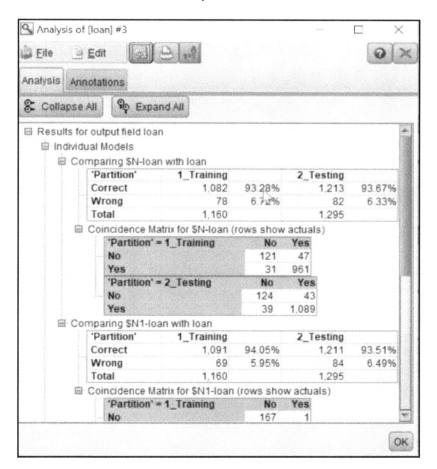

You can see how well we are predicting the No group now! Our model has performed pretty well in predicting the accuracies of the individual models. Hence, we ended up balancing the data, obviously it is at expense of errors in the yes group. But the No group was our matter of concern as it was under-represented.

Summary

This chapter taught us how to modify the various options that are available for enhancing the model. We also learned how to add additional fields and remove noise from these models. Lastly, we sampled the data available, which helped us to understand the model better.

In the next chapter, we are going to learn how to combine models and improve them even further.

5
Advanced Ways of Improving Models

First, we learned to build a model, then we performed diagnostic analysis on it. Then, we determined how accurate the model was, and in this chapter, we will extend our model-building skills. We will learn how to not view a model as an endpoint, but as a starting position to move forward toward improving models. Basically, we will learn how to improve individual models by building more than one model. We have several ways in which we can do that, and we are going to talk about them in detail.

The topics that will be covered in this chapter are as follows. These are also the ways in which we can improve individual models:

- Combining models
- Propensity scores
- Meta-level modeling
- Error modeling
- Boosting and bagging
- Continuous outcomes

Combining models

There are several ways in which models can be combined. We are going to look at each method in this section.

Combining by voting

Let's use an example to understand this method of combining models.

Consider that we have run three models and created a table like this:

Model 1 Prediction	Model 1 Confidence	Model 2 Prediction	Model 2 Confidence	Model 3 Prediction	Model 3 Confidence	Combined Prediction	Final Confidence
Leave	.80	Leave	.70	Leave	.60	Leave	.70
Leave	.80	Leave	.80	Stay	.90	Leave	.53

We have the confidence for each model and its prediction. Let's see how we can combine these models.

If we take a look at the first row, we can see that each of these models is predicting that a person is going to leave. Hence, if we combine the predictions, we are still predicting that the person is going to leave. The confidence value, or the final confidence, is acquired by adding up the confidence values of all the models and dividing by the number of total models, three in our case.

If we look at the second row, we can see that two of these models predict that the person is going to leave; and one model is predicting that the person is going to stay; we can infer that the combined prediction will be that the person will leave. Here, we calculate the confidence values by adding up the confidence of the models that predicted the combined prediction, **Leave**, divided by the total number of models, which is three. Hence, the final confidence value is low in the second row.

This is combining models by voting, where only the predictions that occur a number of times are considered for combining.

Combining by highest confidence

This is another method of combining models. Consider the following table, for example:

Model 1 Prediction	Model 1 Confidence	Model 2 Prediction	Model 2 Confidence	Model 3 Prediction	Model 3 Confidence	Combined Prediction	Final Confidence
Leave	.80	Leave	.70	Leave	.60	Leave	.80
Leave	.80	Leave	.80	Stay	.90	Stay	.90

In this example, we won't consider what the model is predicting; instead, we will just focus on high confidence values. If we look at the first row, each of the models has predicted **Leave**. But **Model 1** has the highest confidence, and so the combined prediction is taken as **Leave** and the final confidence is the highest confidence acquired.

If we look at the second row, the model with highest confidence is **Model 3** and it has predicted that the person is going to stay, and hence, the combined prediction becomes **Stay** and the final confidence becomes the highest confidence.

Implementing combining models

Follow these steps to see how we can combine different models:

1. Get **Electronics_Data** on Canvas.
2. Connect the dataset to a **Partition** node from the **Field Ops** palette.
3. Split the data into training and testing datasets, we have done before.
4. Connect the **Partition** node to the **Neural Net** model and run this model with a random seed set to 5000 and run it.
5. We will now build a **support vector machine** (**SVM**) model. As we are heading towards combining models, we will go to the **Partition** node and connect it with an **SVM** model from the **Modeling** palette.
6. Run the **SVM** model by recalling the edits we had made in the **Expert** tab from Chapter 2, *Getting Started with Machine Learning*. Go to the **Expert** tab, select the mode as **Expert**. Change the **Regularization parameter**, **C** and set it to 5, the middle value, and change the **Kernel** type to **Polynomial**, as that's what gave us an accurate and consistent model earlier on using the same data. Also, change the **Degree** value to 2. We are changing the parameters to these values because we acquired proper results earlier when we first saw a demonstration of this model in Chapter 2, *Getting Started with Machine Learning*. Click on **Run**.
7. Connect both the **SVM** and the **Neural Net** model that were generated.
8. Go to the **Output** palette and connect the generated **SVM** model to a **Table**.

9. Run the table using the **Run** icon on top. You will see the following:

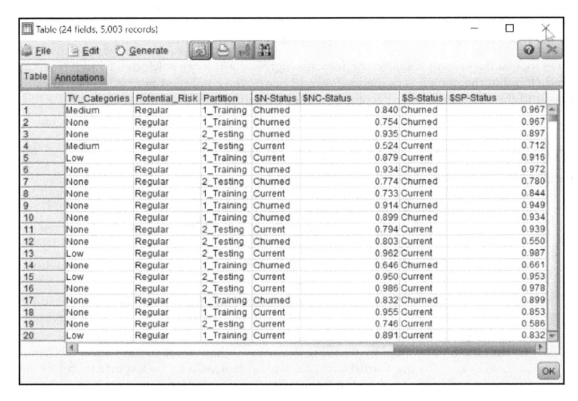

In this, you can see the results from the partition node, the predictions from the **Neural Net** model, its confidence, and even the predictions from the **SVM** model and its confidence. You can close this window.

10. We will now analyze the model by connecting the **SVM**-generated model to an **Analysis** node from the **Output** palette.

11. Edit the **Analysis** node, check the **Coincidence matrices**, and click on **Run**. You will see the following results:

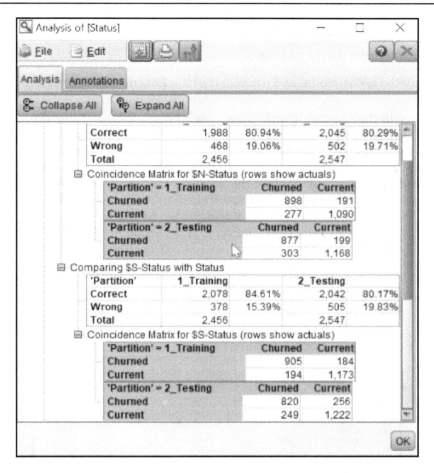

We can see how well each of the models has performed. If you scroll down, you can see that the models have agreed 88% of the time on predictions in the training dataset, and about 87% of the time in the testing dataset. When these models agreed, they were actually correct a fair amount of the time. This brings us to evaluate the possibility of combining these two models.

We are now moving on to combine the models. We will first combine using Modeler, but we will also see how we can combine models outside of a modeler.

Combining models in Modeler

For combining models within a modeler, follow these steps:

1. Go to the **SVM** model and connect it to the **Ensemble** node from the **Field Ops** palette.

2. Let's edit the **Ensemble** node. The **Ensemble** node knows that it is combining the results of two models as it shows two models in ensemble. Choose the **Target field for Ensemble** as the **Status** from the drop-down button on the right. If the **Filter out fields generated by ensemble models** is checked, it will filter out the already generated fields from the previous models, hence, we will deselect it. Next, select the **Ensemble method.** This is a list 0f ways in which we can combine the model. Here, we will select **Voting** as we have already seen this. We will talk about the propensity scores later on in this chapter. Then we have to select what happens when there is a tie; here, we will select **Highest confidence** as we have seen this too and click on **OK**, as shown in the following screenshot:

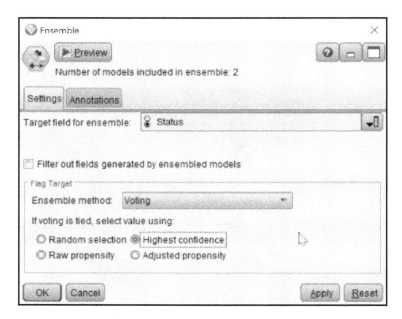

3. Let's see the results of our combination. For this, connect the **Ensemble** node to the **Analysis** node and click on the **Run** button on top. The following will be the results:

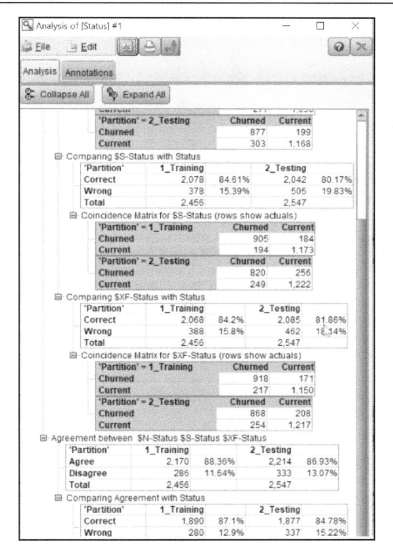

First, we have the results of the **Neural Net** model, followed by the results of the **SVM** model and then finally, we can see the results of the combined model.

We can see that the overall accuracy in the testing dataset is 82%, which means that there is a slight improvement. We were able to improve the accuracy by combining two models by 2% which is great as a starting point. Let's see how we can combine models from outside of Modeler.

Combining models outside Modeler

This method can be used when you are using any data-mining software other than SPSS Modeler.

Let's see how to do that:

1. Go to the **Field Ops** palette and connect the **SVM**-generated model to a **Derive** node.

2. We will use the **Derive** node to create a new field. We will edit this node and name it `Combined_Prediction`.

3. Derive this field as a **Conditional**. You will see an `if-else` condition.

4. Let's tell Modeler that if the predictions from all the models are equal then the combined prediction will be that prediction itself. To do this, let's add an expression in the first `if` condition as, the prediction from the **Neural Net** model, **$N-Status** select **=** the prediction of the **SVM** model, **$S-Status**; go to the `Then` condition, click on the expression builder and select, the prediction of the **Neural Net** model, **$N-Status** or alternatively, you can even select a prediction from the **SVM** model.

5. Write in the `Else` condition, this statement: You can select the variable names from the list:

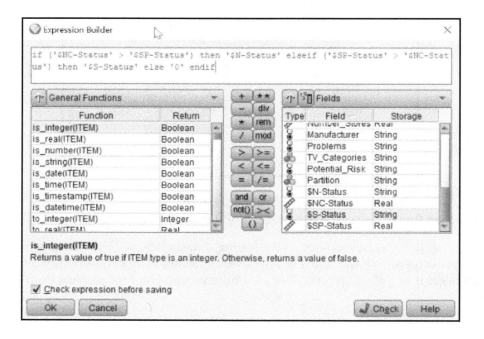

This statement means that we will select the **Highest confidence** from any of the models if the predictions of the two models do not match. And if the confidence of the prediction from the **Neural Net** model is higher than that of the **SVM** model, then we will go with the prediction of the **Neural Net** model. Otherwise, if the confidence of the prediction of the **SVM** model is higher than the **Neural Net** model, then we will go with the **SVM** model. But, if both the conditions don't satisfy, then we will put a `0`, and then we have to end with an `endif` statement. Click on **OK**.

6. Connect the **Combined_prediction** node to the **Table** mode and let's see the results take a look at the results, as shown in the following screenshot:

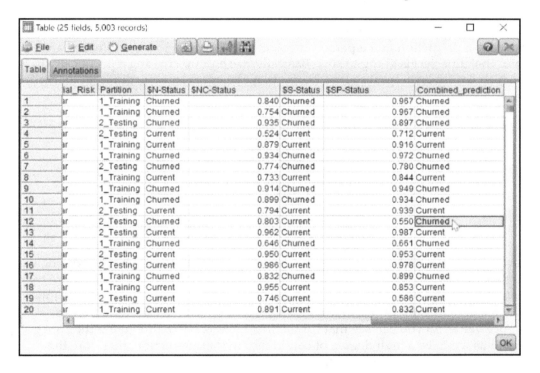

Here, in the 12th row, we can see that the neural network predicted a customer as **Churned** whereas the **SVM** predicted it as **Current**, but as the confidence of the **Neural Net** prediction was higher, the combined prediction was picked as **Churned**.

7. You can analyze this model and see for yourself that the numbers that will be acquired will be similar to the numbers that we had using the **Ensemble** node.

This is how we combined two models to improve accuracy and we saw how we can get the combined results from the two models. You can try this out with three or more models. You will be amazed at how well combining models can work. We will now see another advanced method to improve the model.

Using propensity scores

Propensity scores are very useful because they tell you the likelihood of something happening. Confidence values for models reflect confidence in our predictions so a high degree of confidence doesn't help us determine if we're going to have a customer that's going to stay or leave a company, instead it indicates the confidence that we have in our prediction. Sometimes it's helpful to modify the confidence value so that a high confidence value means a prediction that a person is going to leave and a low confidence value indicates that a person is going to stay. Basically, we end up creating a propensity to leave score which would be helpful so that we could make interventions, different marketing efforts, and so on.

Consider this table, for example:

Prediction	Confidence	Propensity
Leave	.95	.95
Leave	.60	.60
Stay	.55	.45
Stay	.90	.10

We have two values for **Leaving** and two values for **Staying**, each with the confidence values that we have in those predictions. In this example, let's assume that we are trying to calculate the propensity of losing a customer. We will create a propensity score; this means that when a person is predicted to leave, the propensity score is the same thing as a confidence value. So you can see that for the first person, we're predicting they are going to leave, and as we have a high degree of confidence in that prediction, therefore the propensity score is pretty high. For the second person, we're predicting they are also going to leave, but the confidence in that prediction is not quite as high, so therefore, we can see that the propensity score is not quite so high either.

While predicting the opposite, if we are predicting that a third person is going to stay but the confidence in that prediction is not very great, really what we're doing is taking 1 minus the confidence value of the opposite of what we really want, and that ends up being the propensity score. Finally, in the last example, we have a person that we're predicting is going to stay. The confidence in that prediction is extremely high, so therefore, the likelihood of that person leaving is very low.

The following figure sums up the propensity formulas:

○ Propensity = Confidence (for group of interest)
○ Propensity = 1 − Confidence (for the other group)

In essence, what propensity scores do is modify confidence values so that you can see the likelihood of something happening. So, if you could put them all on some kind of spectrum it would be possible to see, for example, that there are some people for whom there is a high degree of confidence that they are going to leave, so maybe there's not much that we can do about that. We have another group of people for whom we have a high degree of confidence that they're going to stay, so the propensity of them leaving is pretty low. Again, we may not necessarily need to worry about them that much, but maybe the people we need to focus on are the people in the middle, because they're the predictions that are not quite as extreme, and so we cannot be quite as confident about those predictions. Potentially, we can do something with that group. We might be able to change their minds, or something like that, and that's how propensity scores can be used.

Implementations of propensity scores

To see how we can use propensity scores to our advantage, follow these steps:

1. Get your dataset on the canvas and connect it to a **Partition** node, dividing the dataset into two parts.
2. Connect the **Partition** node to a **Chaid** model from the **Modeling** tab. You could use any model here, but let's use this as it will be used in our next example as well.

3. **Chaid** will build a decision tree model. To edit, go to the **Model Options** tab, where there is a section that asks for **Propensity Scores**. There are two types; a raw propensity score is for the training dataset and the adjusted propensity score is for the testing or validation dataset. We will select the raw propensity score for now:

4. Click on **Run**. Connect the generated model to a **Table** node from the **Output** palette and run the **Table**. Observe the **Table** and see that we have another variable added known as the propensity score, and when a customer is predicted to be churned, and if their confidence score is low, the propensity score is *1-confidence* of what we really want. But for the **Current** customer, we have a propensity score similar to the confidence value.

5. If you wish to see a graphical representation of this, connect the generated model, to the **Histogram** node from the **Graphs** palette. Edit the **Histogram**, in the field box, and select the propensity score variable:

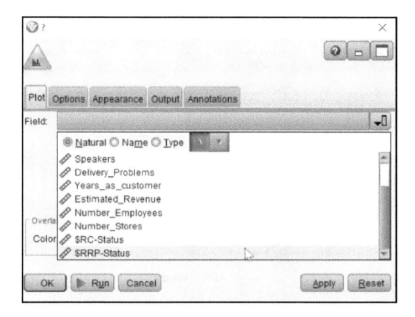

6. Click on **Run** to see the following:

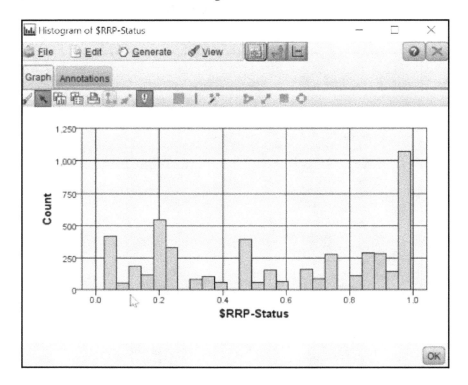

Notice that the propensity scores will range from **0.0** to **1.0**. But the confidence values have only two values, and they have a range from **0.5** to **1.0.** To see this again, go to the histogram and from the **Fields** option, select the **Confidence** variable, then click on **Run**. You will see the following:

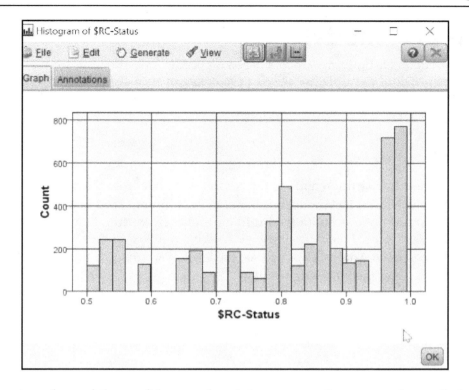

Hence, we transformed the confidence values into a propensity score and now that propensity score is giving us information about the likelihood, in this case, of somebody staying as a customer. We could have done it the other way, where we were finding the propensity score for the likelihood of losing a customer, but we could just invert those scores and it would end up creating that for us. In any case, we can use those propensity scores now to do something with them, to see which customers are the most likely ones that we're going to lose, for example, or those which we're going to keep. However you want to look at it, you know which people that are very likely to be lost and so it may not be possible to do anything with them. Those people that were in the middle might not be lost, so maybe a little more could be done for them to try to keep them as customers and try to understand them better.

Meta-level modeling

Meta-level modeling is building a model based on predictions or results from another model. In the previous example, we saw how to create propensity scores for our **Chaid** model. In this section, we will see how you can extract results from the **Chaid** model and feed them into a **Neural Net** model, and this will enable us to improve the results from a **Neural Net** model.

To do this, follow these steps:

1. Connect the partition node to the **Neural Net** node from the modeling palette.
2. Run the **Neural Net** model by changing the **Random seed** to 5000 from the **Advanced** options under the **Build** tab and click on **Run.** Now connect the generated Chaid model to the generated Neural Net model.
3. Now, use the **Analysis** node to see the level of accuracy of these models.
4. You will get the following results:

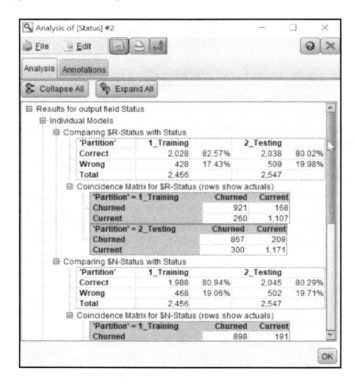

We can see that the accuracy of both the models is somewhat similar, so now we will move on to build a different kind of **Neural Net** model.

We will take the results from the **Chaid** model and feed them to the **Neural Net** model. The **Neural Net** model will then use the results, along with all other individual predictors, to try to capture more than **Chaid**:

1. Right-click on the generated **Neural Net** model and delete it.
2. Connect the generated **Chaid** model to a **Type** node from the **Field Ops** palette.
3. Scroll the **Type** node edit box to the bottom and set the confidence value variable of the **Chaid** model to **None**:

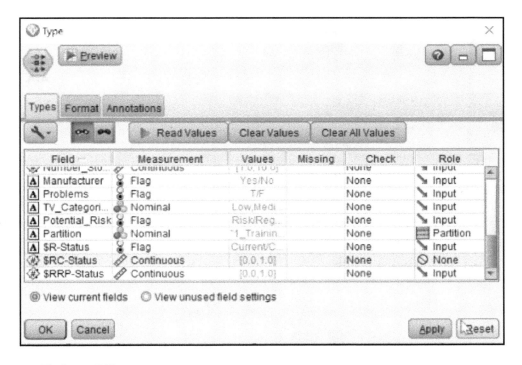

Click on **OK.**

4. Connect the **Type** node to the **Neural Net** model that we already have on the canvas and run it using the **Random seed** of 5000.

5. If you take a look at the results of the new model, you can see that the most important predictors are the propensity scores from the **Chaid** model:

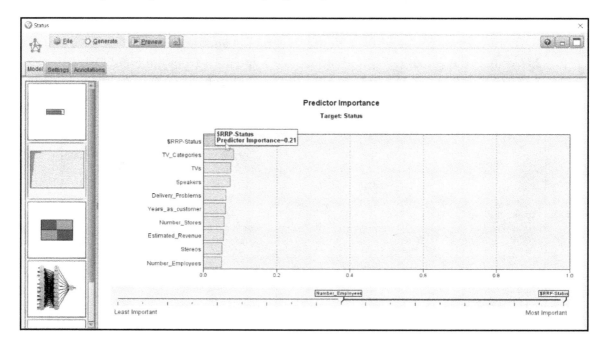

6. Connect the the generated **Chaid** model to **Analysis** node and run the analysis to get the following result:

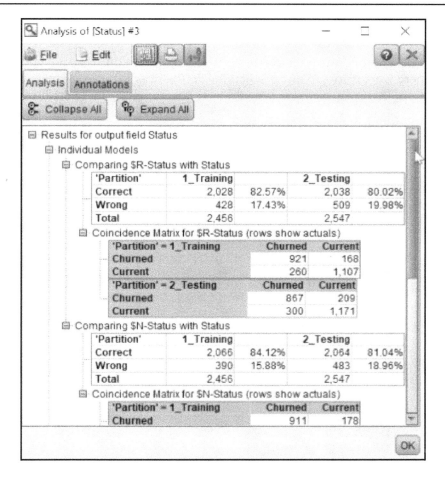

In this example, we can see that in the **Neural Net** model, we got a 1% increase in accuracy if we fed the results from the **Chaid** model.

Error modeling

Error modeling is another form of meta-level modeling but in this case we will be modeling cases where there were errors in our predictions. In this way, we can increase the accuracy of that prediction. Using an example, we will walk through how to do error modeling.

Consider the following scenario, for example:

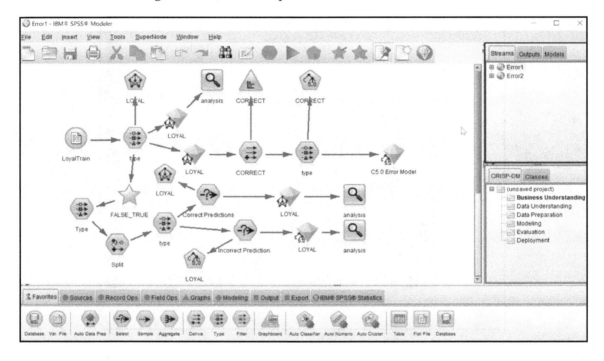

Here, we have a dataset named `LoyalTrain`. This is just a training dataset; we have our testing and validation dataset at a different place and will build a model only on the training dataset. Theer is also a **Type** node and a **Neural Net** model, where we are predicting the variable **loyal**. Run the **Analysis** node to see the results as shown in the following screenshot:

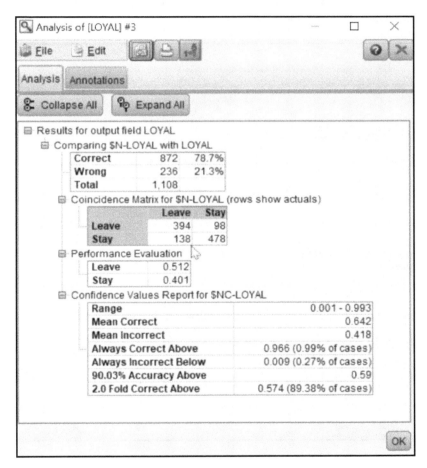

You can see that there are two categories in the outcome variable: people are either predicted to stay or to leave. You can also see that correct predictions were made in 79% of the cases. Mistakes were made in 21% of the cases. In total, there were 236 errors.

From this example, you can also see that the **Neural Net** model was copied and placed in another part of the stream. A new variable, CORRECT, was also made using a **Derive** node. Let's take a look at what's happened here, as shown in the following screenshot:

Here, we have created a new field as CORRECT, and we have kept its values as True and False. We are telling Modeler here that if it finds a variable, **LOYAL**, and if it is equal to the prediction of **LOYAL**, then the value is **True**; otherwise, it is **False**.

If you run the **Distribution** node placed above it, you will see the following results:

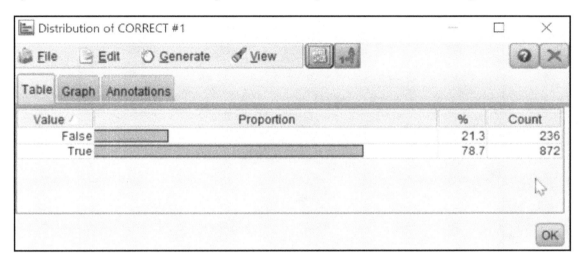

Next, we will use the **Type** node to instantiate the data, after which we can use a **C5.0** decision tree model that looks at the data in a very different way. Here we have built a **C5.0** model that is trying to predict if we are getting a correct or an incorrect prediction. Click on the generated **C5.0** model to see its results, as shown in the following screenshot:

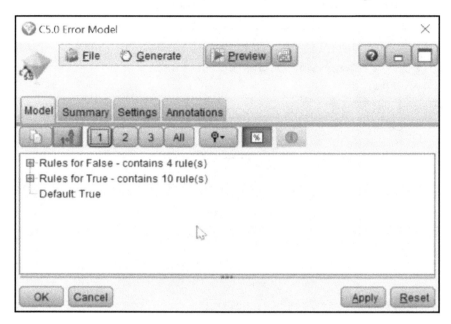

In this example, we can see that we have 14 rows with **4 rule(s)** for a **False** prediction, that is, when we are predicting incorrectly, and **10 rule(s)** for **True** values when we are predicting correctly.

You can expand the rules and click on the % sign above them to get the following results:

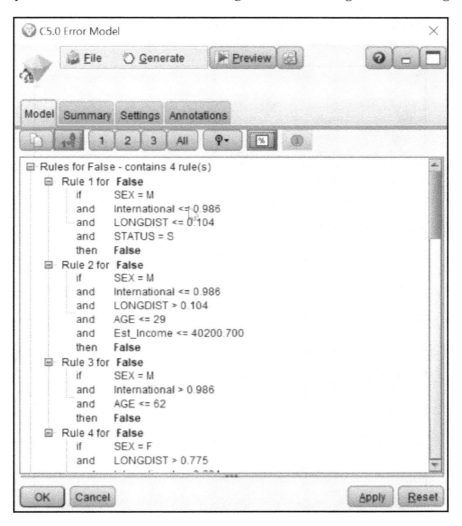

In this example, the first rule basically states that if you're male and you're using fewer than 1 minute of international calls, fewer than 1 minute of long-distance calls, and your status is single, we are predicting that we will have a value of **False**. If you want to see the numbers, click on the % sign, where you will see the following results:

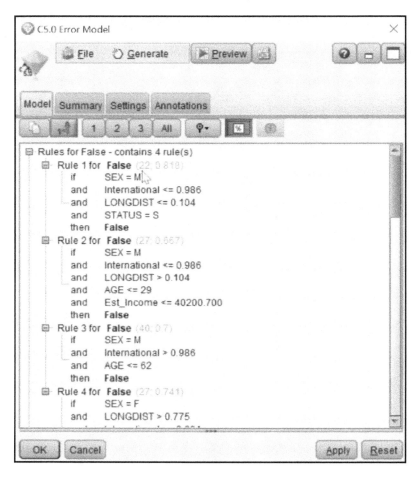

As shown in the preceding screenshot, first rule had 22 people, and the accuracy of predictions relating to them was around 82%.

From this, we can see that there are certain kinds of mistakes cropping up while we are making the predictions. We might therefore need to use another kind of model instead of a **Neural Net** model. To do this, click on the **Generate** option and select the **Rule Trace Node**, as shown in the following screenshot:

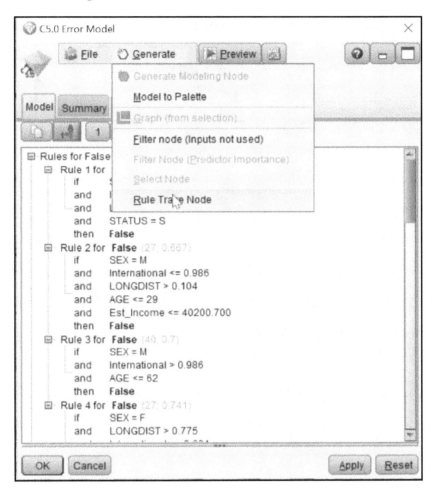

This step created the **FALSE_TRUE** node that you can see in the example scenario as the Start icon. This creates all of our rules. If you wish to take a look inside it, click on the Start + icon on the **Tools** tab, where you should see the following result:

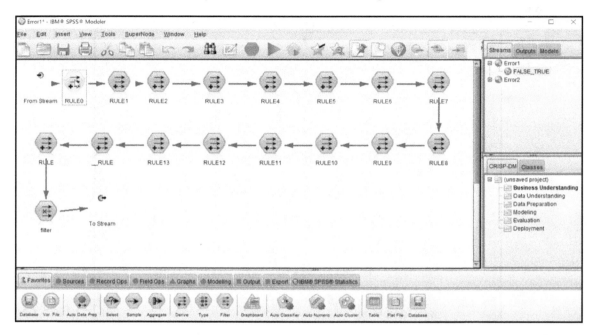

Let's now take a look at the first rule. Click on the expression builder in that rule, as shown in the following screenshot:

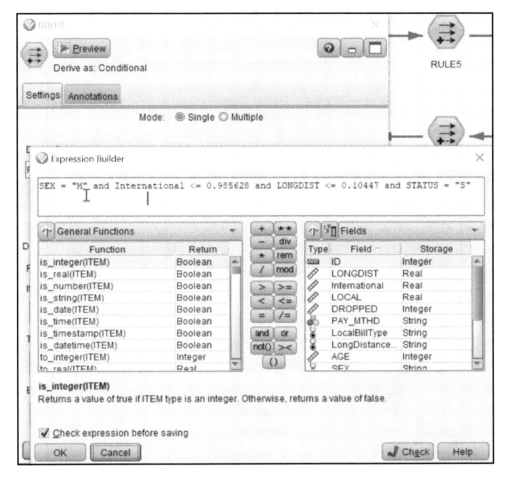

Here, the rule appears to state that if you're male and you're using fewer than 1 minute of international calls, fewer than 1 minute of long-distance calls, and your status is also single, we're predicting that you're going to have a value of **False**. You can see the accuracy in that prediction.

Go back using the Start icon. Here, we have the classify node, `Split`. Let's see what we have done so far, as follows:

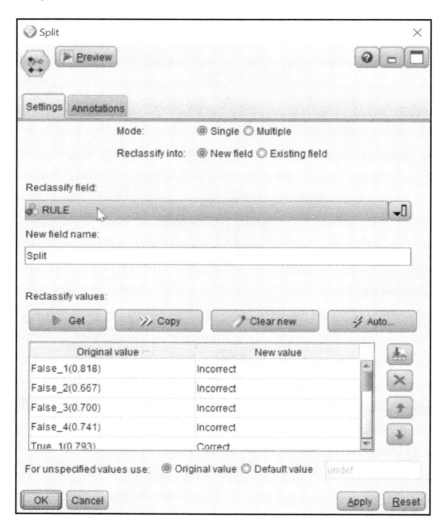

We have taken the variable **RULE** and clicked on **Get**, which gave us all of these different original values of **False**, which we renamed to **Incorrect** and all the values of **True**, which were renamed to **Correct**, and then we had just the **Correct Predictions**:

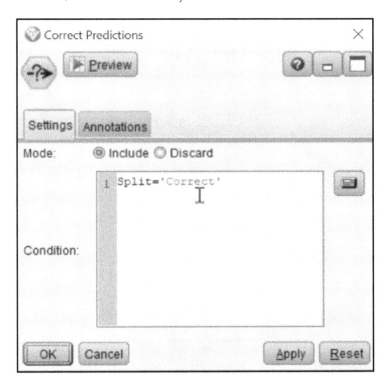

We have now built the **Neural Net** model. If you run the **Analysis** node of the generated **Neural Net** model from the **Correct Predictions**, you should see the following results:

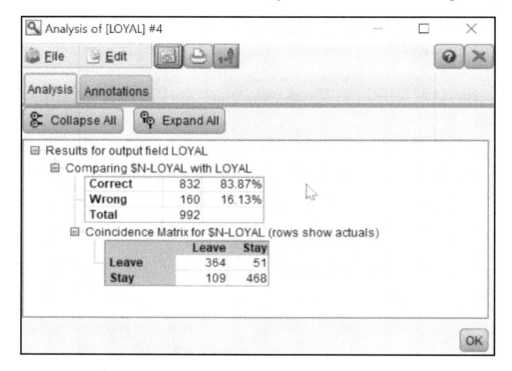

Remember that the overall accuracy of the earlier model was around 79%, which has now improved to around 84%.

We have also done the same thing for incorrect predictions in a separate field from the **Type** node. Let's have a look at that, as follows:

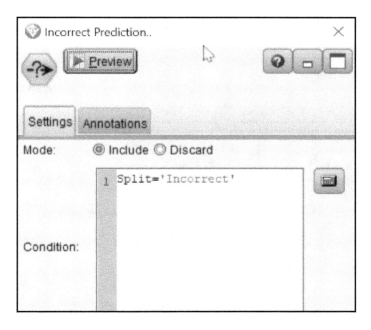

We built a **C5.0** model for incorrect predictions, so let's take a look at its analysis, as follows:

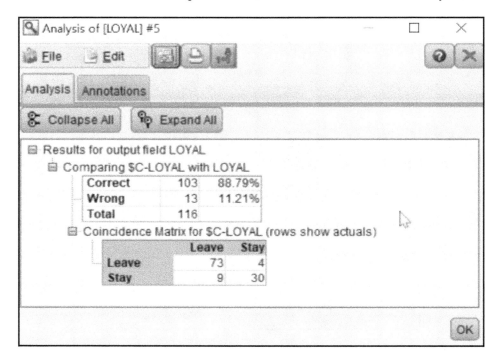

The **C5.0** model has done a great job at predicting the incorrect values where the **Neural Net** model didn't work well; we now have an overall accuracy of 89%.

Let's sum up what we did here. We had a dataset that we split into correct and incorrect results and separately modeled each one to give us fewer errors than we used one model.

Now we need to combine the predictions from the two models. For this, go to the **Error 2** Stream from the **Streams** tab at the right, as shown in the following screenshot:

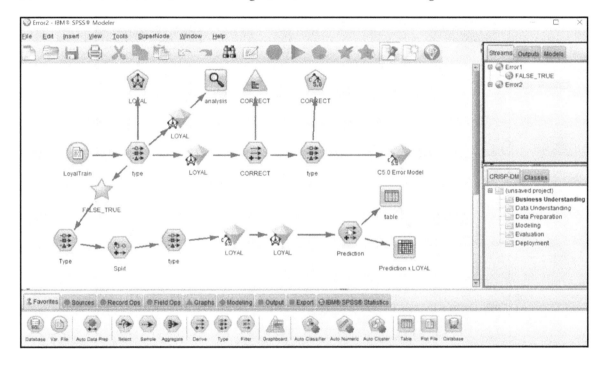

Here, we have combined the predictions of both the models and have used a **Derive** node **Prediction**, as shown in the following screenshot:

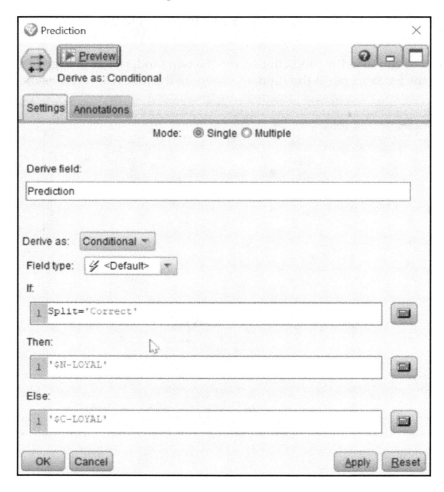

Here, we have specified that if a prediction is correct, the prediction of the **Neural Net** model should be opted for. If a prediction is incorrect, we should opt for the prediction of the **C5.0** model.

Then, having added the **Matrix** node, run the following:

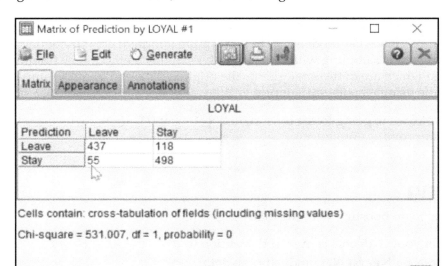

What we can see in the preceding screenshot is that we have correctly predicted that **437** people will leave with **118** errors, and that **498** people will stay with just **55** errors. This means there is a total number of 173 errors.

Our original model made 236 errors, so we have brought down the number of errors by a great extent. Just by using two different models for different groups of people and by combining them with, we have produced an output with 63 fewer errors.

This is error modeling. In error modelling you can build one model, see what the results look like, and then decide from there whether to build two or three models for different types of people, because it can't be assumed that one size fits all. Therefore, we can build different kinds of models, feed different types of data to those models, and then ultimately combine the results of each model to produce a final prediction that can end up having fewer errors in terms of the predictive modeling undertaken.

Boosting and bagging

The idea behind boosting is that by building successive models that are built to predict the misclassifications of earlier models you're performing a form of error modeling. Bagging, on the other hand, is sampling with replacement. With this method, new training datasets are generated which are of the same size as the original dataset. For our example in this section, will be using a bootstrap sample.

In this example, we're going to see how to do boosting and bagging, which are two methods of improving a model.

Boosting

Let's see how to do boosting with the following steps:

1. Get your data on a canvas and partition it.
2. Create a **Neural Net** model for the data.
3. Run the **Neural Net** model with a **Random seed** set to `5000`.
4. Connect an **Analysis** node and run it with **Coincidence matrices** checked – you will see that the testing accuracy is 81% and the overall accuracy is 80%.
5. Now, boost the **Neural Net** model. For this, go to the **Neural Net** model and edit it. Go to **Objectives** under **Build options** and click on **Enhance model accuracy** (boosting). Boosting can be used with any size of dataset. The idea here is that we're building successive models that are built to predict the misclassifications of earlier models. So, basically, we end up building a model. There'll be some errors, so a second model should be built where the errors of the first model are given more weight so that we're able to understand them better. Then, when we build a second model, there are going to be errors, so we end up building a third model where the errors of the second model are given more weight again so that we try to understand them better, and so forth. Whenever you're doing boosting and bagging, you always have to make sure you have a training and a testing dataset because there's a very good chance that you're going to capitalize on chance, and that you might find sample-specific information because we're focusing on the errors that we're finding within that specific sample. We'll now click on **Run**.

6. Let's take a look at our generated model:

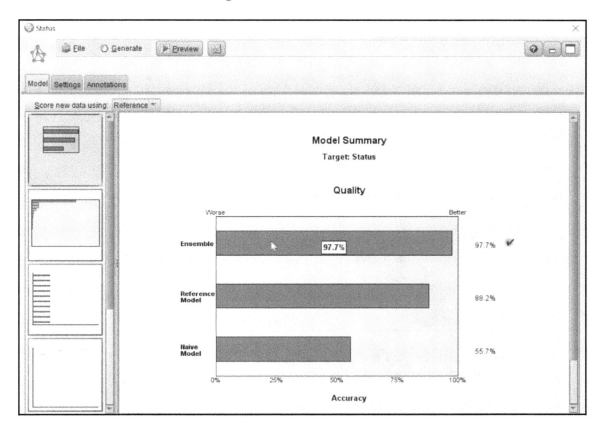

The first tab that we have here in our generated model is showing us what the Ensemble model looks like: that's combining the 10 models that we've created. You can see its overall accuracy is about 98%: that's the model that's been chosen as the best model. You can also see what the reference model is—that would be the first model that was built—and then you can see the naive model and, really, that's no model, that's just where we're predicting the mode or the most common response.

7. Let's go down to the second icon:

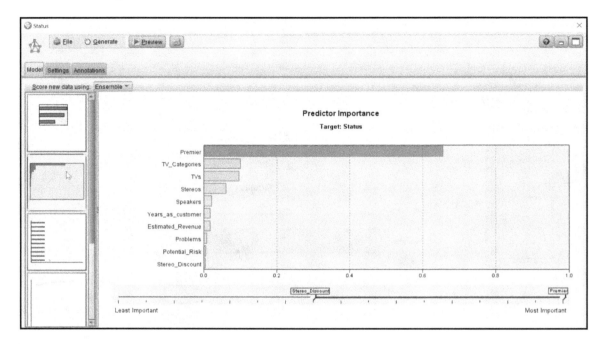

Here, you can see the **Predictor Importance**. Across the 10 models that we ended up building, we can see that the **Premier** variable was the most important predictor and then you can see what the other predictors were in terms of their order of importance. This is the same kind of information that we would see typically with a general **Neural Net** model, but this information comes from across all the different models that we built.

8. If we go down to the next icon we can see **Predictor Frequency**:

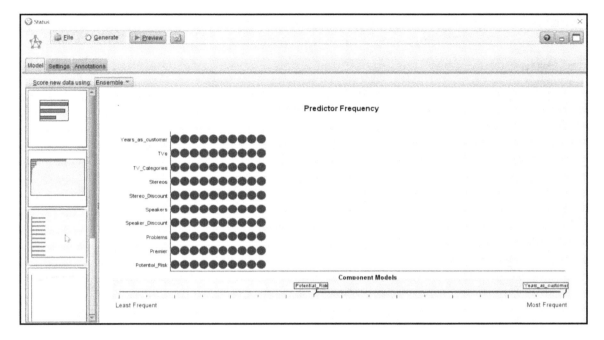

This shows us how frequently each one of the different predictors was used in the model. For a **Neural Net** model this is not so interesting because **Neural Net** models generally do not drop predictors, but if we had a decision tree model, for example, this could be a little more interesting because there you do drop predictors.

9. Let's go down to the next tab:

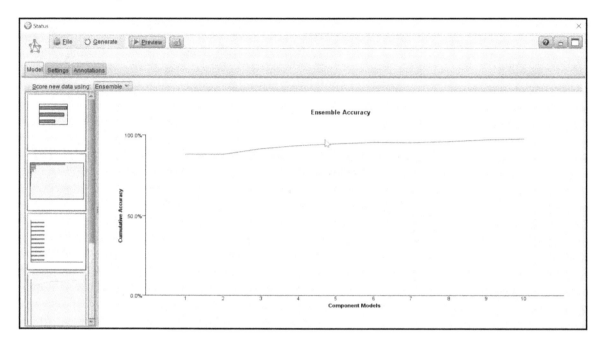

The preceding screenshot is showing us the level of accuracy of the model. You can see that it flattens out and, at some point, there's no longer much of an improvement. In this case, it's a gradual increase in terms of accuracy. Sometimes, in some models, you see perhaps five models that there's a huge jump in accuracy and then it just stabilizes. Maybe you wouldn't necessarily need to build any more models. In our case, we ended up building 10 models. Our overall accuracy was extremely high. If we had seen much lower accuracy, perhaps because we saw a gradual increase, maybe we would want to use 15 models instead of 10, for example. That's where you would see this kind of information.

10. Let's scroll down a little further and let's see the final table:

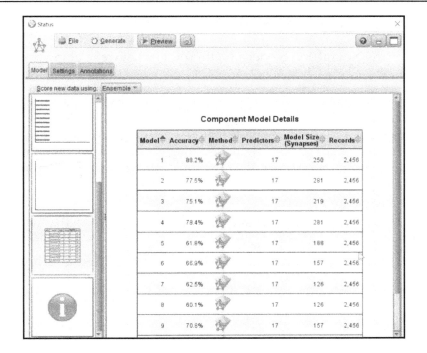

Here, we can see the number of predictors and we can also see the number of cases that we had in the model as well. Finally, we see the number of synapses, which are basically the number of weights or the number of connections that we have within this model. So, you can see how well each one of these individual models is doing. Each new version of a model is giving more weight to where we had more errors in the data and that's basically the idea here.

11. Run the **Analysis** node, finally, and you can see that for the training dataset the overall accuracy was about 98%. But in the testing dataset the overall accuracy was about 80% that's what we really care about, the testing dataset. In this case, we see that there's a big difference between training and testing and that's generally going to be the situation when talking about boosting models.

Make sure that whatever result you get is really worth it, and that it's really an improvement over just running the model on its own. In this case, when we just ran one model, remember that the overall accuracy on the testing data set was at about 80%; that's what we have here. So really, boosting didn't do much for us in this particular situation. In other situations, it certainly can, but again you want really to be able to weigh that, and in this case boost seemed to be probably not really worth it for us in this situation.

Bagging

Let's go back into the **Neural Net** model and, this time, what we're going to do is bagging instead of boosting:

1. Go over to the **Objectives** tab and select **Enhance model stability** – it's sampling with replacement. Do not do bagging when you have small datasets or outliers. The main idea behind bagging is that new training datasets are generated that are of the same size as the original training dataset and this is done by using sampling with replacement. We're actually bootstrapping in this kind of situation.

2. Click on **Run** for the model.

3. Let's take a look at our generated model. This is the model that we ended up building:

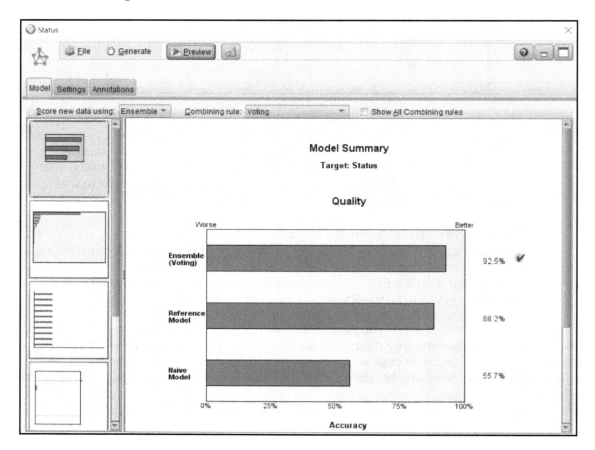

Notice that the combining rule is achieved by voting but there are other ways in which we can combine models and, in fact, we can choose the option to show all the combining rules. We won't see the details for all the models because the screenshots are the same as with boosting.

4. Run the **Analysis** node to get the following results:

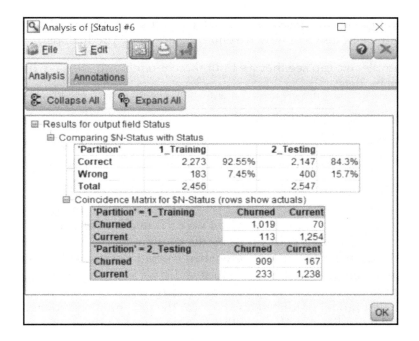

We can see that, by doing the bagging, we got a 4% increase in accuracy.

We will now see how to predict continuous outcomes.

Predicting continuous outcomes

Until now, we have spent all of our time talking about categorical outcomes and most of those examples apply to continuous outcomes, but in this section we're going to focus exclusively on continuous outcome variables.

As I mentioned previously, when we're talking about continuous outcome predictions or variables, everything that we've talked about in this book still applies: the main difference, though, is going to be in terms of how we end up combining predictions.

Here, in this example, we can see that we built three models and we have predictions from each one of those models:

Model 1 Prediction	Model 2 Prediction	Model 3 Prediction	Combined Prediction
7	9	8	8
12.5	12.5	12.5	12.5
10	9	8.5	9.167
2	3	10	5

When we want to combine the predictions, all we do is take a mathematical average. The mean of these previous models ends up being the combined prediction because we're not predicting individual categories as we were when we had a categorical outcome variable. Instead, we're predicting actual numeric values and if we want to combine predictions from these different models, all we do, simply, is take the average of the models. For example, in the first row, the first model predicted a value of **7**, the next model predicted a value of **9**, and the third model predicted **8**. We take those values, we add them up, we divide them by the number of models, and the combined prediction ends up being a value of **8**. That's the way you would combine your models.

But when we have continuous outcome variables, we do not have a confidence value, so we don't need to worry about the actual confidence values for those kind of models.

In this example, we're going to use the bank dataset. Bring it onto the canvas.

Let's just take a look at what that data looks like:

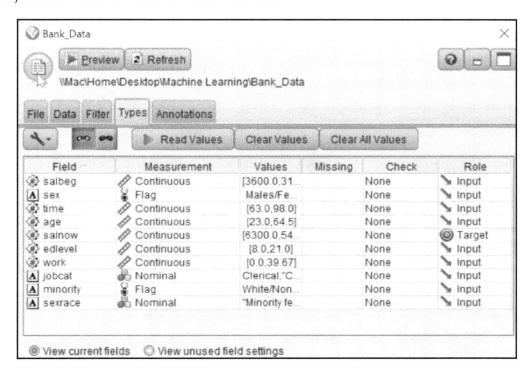

As you can see, there are several fields. We will predict a variable, **salnow**, that's our target variable based on a beginning salary, gender, the amount of time that someone has worked at this organization, their age, their level of education, the number of years that they have worked prior to coming to this organization, the job category that they're in, whether they're from a minority, and then the interaction of race and gender.

Partition the dataset and go on to create a **Neural Net** model. Run the **Neural Net** model with default settings. Take a look at the newly generated model.

Let's also build the **SVM** model just as we have done before. We will compare the results of both the models.

This is the output for the **SVM** model:

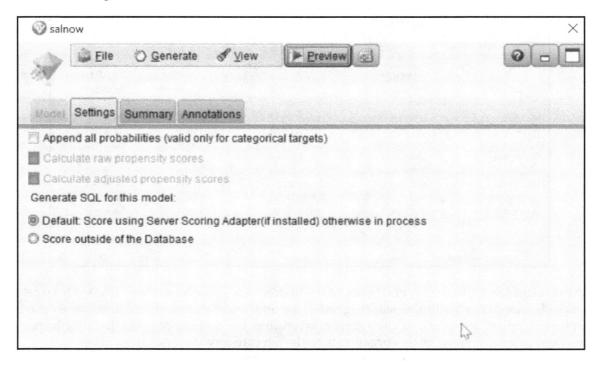

Connect the two generated models and connect the **SVM** model to a **Table** and run the table.
Scroll towards the end and you can see a **Partition** node and predictions of the two models. Notice that there are no confidence values for these continuous outcome variables.

This also means that we won't get the propensity scores for these models either. Bring an **Analysis** node and connect the **SVM** model to the **Analysis** node and run it:

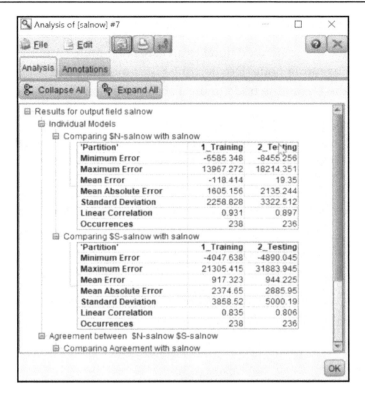

The analysis is a little bit different than what we used to get with the categorical variables. You can see that there is a **Minimum Error**, and a **Maximum Error** for both the training and the testing datasets. The model has done a worst job in over- or under-predicting the values.

Mean Error is just averaging of the errors. The best way to look at the accuracy of these models is by looking at the **Mean Absolute Error**. As you can see, we have a lower value for the training dataset as compared to the testing dataset. These values need to be similar. You can see the mean absolute value for the **SVM** model. You can also see the **Standard Deviation**. This needs to be as small as possible because this shows that we have less variation in the model. Another criterion is the correlation coefficient. That is extremely high for both the datasets; these values must be similar to each other. People use linear coefficients to validate the usefulness of a model, but sometimes we don't have linear relationships. So, in such cases, we will use the mean absolute error value as the best measure of assessing how the model is performing. **Occurrences** are the number of cases that we have for each dataset.

Let's now combine the model:

1. Connect the last generated node to an ensemble node from the **Field Ops** palette.
2. Edit the **Ensemble** node. Deselect the **Filter out** field and click **OK**.
3. Connect the **Ensemble** node to the **Table** node already present and run the **Table**.
4. You can see that we have predictions from the **SVM**, **Neural Net**, and if we average those two, we have the predictions from the combined model. We also have our standard errors as well. For those who are not using modeler, a **Derive** node can be used to calculate the averages of these models and get a combined result.
5. To see the results, connect the **Ensembles** node to an **Analysis** node and run it:

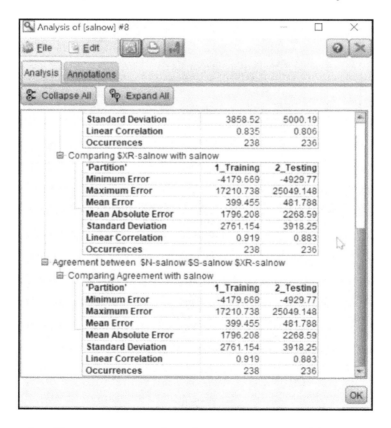

This was an example of how we can work with continuous variables.

Summary

In this chapter, we saw how we can make additional advance operations on models to get better results. Hopefully, you have a deeper insight into how data is fetched to train a machine and how we can make a better model by training it on different types of data.

Other Books You May Enjoy

If you enjoyed this book, you may be interested in these other books by Packt:

Mastering Machine Learning Algorithms
Giuseppe Bonaccorso

ISBN: 9781788621113

- Explore how a ML model can be trained, optimized, and evaluated
- Understand how to create and learn static and dynamic probabilistic models
- Successfully cluster high-dimensional data and evaluate model accuracy
- Discover how artificial neural networks work and how to train, optimize, and validate them
- Work with Autoencoders and Generative Adversarial Networks
- Apply label spreading and propagation to large datasets
- Explore the most important Reinforcement Learning techniques

Python Machine Learning By Example - Second Edition
Yuxi (Hayden) Liu

ISBN: 9781789616729

- Understand the important concepts in machine learning and data science
- Use Python to explore the world of data mining and analytics
- Scale up model training using varied data complexities with Apache Spark
- Delve deep into text and NLP using Python libraries such NLTK and gensim
- Select and build an ML model and evaluate and optimize its performance
- Implement ML algorithms from scratch in Python, TensorFlow, and scikit-learn

Leave a review - let other readers know what you think

Please share your thoughts on this book with others by leaving a review on the site that you bought it from. If you purchased the book from Amazon, please leave us an honest review on this book's Amazon page. This is vital so that other potential readers can see and use your unbiased opinion to make purchasing decisions, we can understand what our customers think about our products, and our authors can see your feedback on the title that they have worked with Packt to create. It will only take a few minutes of your time, but is valuable to other potential customers, our authors, and Packt. Thank you!

Index